5th Workshop on Cross Lingual Information Access 2011

Held at the 5th International Joint Conference on Natural Language Processing 2011 (IJCNLP 2011)

Chiang Mai, Thailand
13 November 2011

ISBN: 978-1-62276-457-0

Printed from e-media with permission by:

Curran Associates, Inc.
57 Morehouse Lane
Red Hook, NY 12571

proceedings.com

Some format issues inherent in the e-media version may also appear in this print version.

Printed by Curran Associates, Inc. (2012)

Association for Computational Linguistics
209 N. Eighth Street
Stroudsburg, Pennsylvania 18360

Phone: 1-570-476-8006
Fax: 1-570-476-0860

acl@aclweb.org

Additional copies of this publication are available from:

Curran Associates, Inc.
57 Morehouse Lane
Red Hook, NY 12571 USA
Phone: 845-758-0400
Fax: 845-758-2634
Email: curran@proceedings.com
Web: www.proceedings.com

Table of Contents

Introduction

Welcome to the IJCNLP-2011 Workshop on *Cross Lingual Information Access:Computational Linguistics and the Information Need of Multilingual Societies*.

The development of digital and online information repositories is creating many opportunities and also new challenges in information retrieval. The availability of online documents in many different languages makes it possible for users around the world to directly access previously unimagined sources of information. However in conventional information retrieval systems the user must enter a search query in the language of the documents in order to retrieve it. This requires that users can express their queries in those languages in which the information is available and can understand the documents returned by the retrieval process. This restriction clearly limits the amount and type of information that an individual user really has access to.

Cross lingual information access (CLIA) is concerned with any technologies and applications that enable people to freely access information that is expressed in any languages. With the rapid development of globalization and digital online information in Internet, huge demand for cross lingual information access has emerged from ordinary netizens (polyglots or monoglots) who are surfing the Internet for special information (e.g. travelling, product description), and communicating in soaring social networks (e.g. Facebook, Youtube, Twitter, Myspace), to global companies which provide multilingual services to their multinational customers, and governments who aim to lower the barriers to international commerce and collaboration, and homeland security. This huge demand has triggered vigorous research and development in CLIA.

In recent times, research in Cross Lingual Information Access has been vigorously pursued through several international fora, such as, the Cross-Language Evaluation Forum (CLEF), NTCIR Asian Language Retrieval, Question-answering Workshop, cross language information retrieval in Indian languages (FIRE) and such other fora. In addition to CLIR, significant results have been obtained in multilingual summarization workshops and cross-language named entity extraction challenges by the ACL (Association for Computational Linguistics) and the Geographic Information retrieval (GeoCLEF) track of CLEF.

This workshop is a continuous effort to address the need of cross-lingual information access on top of its previous four issues which were held during IJCAI 2007 in Hyderabad, IJCNLP 2008 in Hyderabad, NAACL 2009 in Colorado, and COLING 2010 in Beijing. It aims to bring together researchers from a variety of fields such as information retrieval, computational linguistics, machine translation, and digital library, and practitioners from government and industry to address the issues of information need of multilingual society.

This fifth international workshop on Cross Lingual Information Access aims to bring together various trends in multi-source, cross and multilingual information retrieval and access, and provide a venue for researchers and practitioners from academia, government, and industry to interact and share a broad spectrum of ideas, views and applications. This workshop also aims to highlight and emphasize the contributions of Natural Language Processing (NLP) and Computational Linguistics to CLIA. The present workshop includes an invited keynote talk followed by presentations of technical papers selected after peer review.

The workshop starts with an invited keynote talk *Web-based Machine Translation* given by Haifeng Wang.

The technical paper presentations will start from the second session of the workshop. The paper by Knoth *et al* addresses the issue of explicit semantic analysis for cross-lingual link discovery. This paper explores how to automatically generate cross-language links between resources in large document collections.The paper presents new methods that are applicable to any multilingual document collection. They reported a comparative study on the Wikipedia corpus and provide new insights into the evaluation of link discovery systems. In the work of Siva Reddy and Serge Sharoff, they propose cross language PoS taggers for Indian Languages. They show how to build a cross-language PoS tagger for Kannada exploiting the resources of Telugu. In addition they also build large corpora and a morphological analyser for Kannada. They showed that a cross-language taggers are as efficient as mono-lingual taggers. The work by Duo Ding introduces an ongoing work of leveraging a cross-lingual topic model (CLTM) to integrate the multilingual search results. The CLTM detects the underlying topics of different language results and uses the topic distribution of each result to cluster them into topic-based classes. In CLTM, they unify distributions in topic level by direct translation, thus distinguishing from other multi-lingual topic models, which mainly concern the parallelism at document or sentence level. They suggested that CLTM clustering method is effective and outperforms few other existing document clustering techniques. Manaal *et al* propose a soundex-based translation correction in Urdu-English cross-language information retrieval. They discuss the challenges associated with the resource-poor language like Urdu and show the effectiveness of the proposed approach on the benchmark dataset. Li *et al* adopted the contextualized hidden Markov model (CHMM) framework for unsupervised Russian PoS tagging. They propose a backoff smoothing method that incorporates left, right, and unambiguous context into the transition probability estimation during the expectation-maximization process. They show that the resulting model achieves overall and disambiguation accuracies comparable to a CHMM using the classic backoff smoothing method for HMM-based PoS tagging. Johannes Knopp addresses extending a multilingual lexical resource by bootstrapping named entity classification using Wikipedia category system. Their approach is able to classify more than two million named entities and improves the quality of an existing NER resource.

With these diverse of topics, we look forward to a lively exchange of ideas in the workshop.

We thank Haifeng Wang for the invited keynote talk, all the members of the Program Committee for their excellent and insightful reviews, the authors who submitted contributions for the workshop and the participants for making the workshop a success.

Organizing Committee
The 5th International Workshop on Cross Lingual Information Access
IJCNLP 2011
November 13, 2011.

Organizers:

Asif Ekbal, IIT Patna, India (Co-chair)
Deyi Xiong, Institute for InfoComm Research, Singapore (Co-chair)
Prasenjit Majumder, DAIICT, India
Mitesh Khapra, IIT Bombay

Program Committee:

Eneko Agirre, University of the Basque Country
Rafael Banchs, Institute for Infocomm Research
Sivaji Bandyopadhyay, Jadavpur University
Pushpak Bhattacharya, IIT Bombay
Nicola Cancedda, Xerox Research Center
Somnath Chandra, MIT, Govt. of India
Wenliang Chen, Institute for Infocomm Research
Patrick Saint Dizier, IRIT, Universite Paul Sabatier
Xiangyu Duan, Institute for Infocomm Research
Nicola Ferro, University of Padua
Cyril Goutte, National Research Council of Canada
Gareth Jones, Dublin City University
Joemon Jose, University of Glasgow
A Kumaran, Microsoft Research of India
Jun Lang, Institute for Infocomm Research
Swaran Lata, MIT, Govt. of India
Gina-Anne Levow, National Centre for Text Mining (UK)
Qun Liu, Institute of Computing Technology, CAS
Yang Liu, Institute of Computing Technology, CAS
Mandar Mitra, ISI Kolkata
Doug Ouard, University of Maryland, College Park
Carol Peters, Istituto di Scienza e Tecnologie dell'Informazione and CLEF campaign
Paolo Rosso, Technical University of Valencia
Sudeshna Sarkar, IIT Kharagpur
Hendra Setiawan, University of Maryland
L Sobha, AU-KBC, Chennai
Rohini Srihari, University at Buffalo, SUNY
Ralf Steinberger, European Commission - Joint Research Centre, Italy
Le Sun, Institute of Software, CAS
Vasudeva Varma, IIIT Hyderabad
Thuy Vu, Institute for Infocomm Research
Haifeng Wang, Baidu
Yunqing Xia, Tsinghua University, China
Min Zhang, Institute for Infocomm Research
Guodong Zhou, SooChow Universit
Chengqing Zong, Institute of Automation, CAS
Raghavendra Udupa, Microsoft Research

Invited Speaker:

Haifeng Wang, Baidu

We wish to thank our sponsors

Gold Sponsors

www.google.com

www.baidu.com

The Office of Naval Research (ONR)

The Asian Office of Aerospace Research and Development (AOARD)

Department of Systems Engineering and Engineering Managment, The Chinese University of Hong Kong

Silver Sponsors

Microsoft Corporation

Bronze Sponsors

Chinese and Oriental Languages Information Processing Society (COLIPS)

Supporter

Thailand Convention and Exhibition Bureau (TCEB)

We wish to thank our sponsors

Organizers

Asian Federation of Natural Language Processing (AFNLP)

National Electronics and Computer Technology Center (NECTEC), Thailand

Sirindhorn International Institute of Technology (SIIT), Thailand

Rajamangala University of Technology Lanna (RMUTL), Thailand

Maejo University, Thailand

Chiang Mai University (CMU), Thailand

Conference Program

Saturday, November 13, 2011

8:35–8:45	Opening Remarks
8:45–10:00	Keynote Speech
	Web-based Machine Translation Haifeng Wang
10:00–10:30	Break
10:30–11:10	*Using Explicit Semantic Analysis for Cross-Lingual Link Discovery* Petr Knoth, Lukas Zilka and Zdenek Zdrahal
11:10–11:50	*Cross Language POS Taggers (and other Tools) for Indian Languages: An Experiment with Kannada using Telugu Resources* Siva Reddy and Serge Sharoff
11:50–14:00	Lunch
14:00–14:30	*Integrate Multilingual Web Search Results using Cross-Lingual Topic Models* Duo Ding
14:30–15:00	*Soundex-based Translation Correction in Urdu–English Cross-Language Information Retrieval* Manaal Faruqui, Prasenjit Majumder and Sebastian Pado
15:00–15:30	*Unsupervised Russian POS Tagging with Appropriate Context* Li Yang, Erik Peterson, John Chen, Yana Petrova and Rohini Srihari
15:30–16:00	Break
16:00–16:40	*Extending a multilingual Lexical Resource by bootstrapping Named Entity Classification using Wikipedia's Category System* Johannes Knopp
16:40–17:00	Closing

Web-based Machine Translation

Haifeng Wang
Baidu
Beijing, 100085, China
wanghaifeng@baidu.com

1 Abstract

Machine translation (MT) has been studied for more than 60 years. World-Wide-Web offers more opportunities to MT. We could try to crawl more web data to train the MT system. But we have to filter the very noisy web data. There are many potential web-based applications for MT, such as translation of web-page, translation of instant message, translation of SNS, translation of e-commerce, mobile translation, etc. To make better use of the web data, and to produce better web-based MT applications, we should also adapt the MT methods to the web scenario. In this talk, I will introduce our work on web-based machine translation.

2 Biography

Dr. WANG Haifeng a senior scientist at Baidu, and a visiting professor at Harbin Institute of Technology. At Baidu, he is the head of Baidu's NLP department, and the advisor of its speech team, the technical leader of its recommendation & personalization team, and one of the core members of Baidu's technology committee. He received his PhD in computer science from Harbin Institute of Technology in 1999. He worked as an associate researcher at Microsoft Research China 1999 2000, a research scientist at iSilk.com (Hong Kong) 20002002, and chief research scientist and deputy director at Toshiba (China) R&D Center till Jan. 2010. He has authored more than 70 NLP papers, including 13 full papers in ACL main conferences. His research interests span a wide range of topics including: MT (SMT, RBMT, EBMT, TM and hybrid methods), parsing, generation, grammar induction, paraphrase, collocation extraction, SRL, WSD, LM, recommendation, personalization, speech and search. He has served as program chair, area chair, tutorial chair, workshop chair, industry track chair and PC members for numerous NLP conferences including ACL, SIGIR, NAACL, EMNLP, COLING and IJCNLP, etc. He also serves as associate editor of ACM TALIP, guest editor of ACM TIST. He is the Vice-President-Elect of the ACL.

Proceedings of the 5th International Joint Conference on Natural Language Processing, page 1,
Chiang Mai, Thailand, November 8-12, 2011.

Using Explicit Semantic Analysis for Cross-Lingual Link Discovery

Petr Knoth
KMi, The Open University
p.knoth@open.ac.uk

Lukas Zilka
KMi, The Open University
l.zilka@open.ac.uk

Zdenek Zdrahal
KMi, The Open University
z.zdrahal@open.ac.uk

Abstract

This paper explores how to automatically generate cross-language links between resources in large document collections. The paper presents new methods for Cross-Lingual Link Discovery (CLLD) based on Explicit Semantic Analysis (ESA). The methods are applicable to any multilingual document collection. In this report, we present their comparative study on the Wikipedia corpus and provide new insights into the evaluation of link discovery systems. In particular, we measure the agreement of human annotators in linking articles in different language versions of Wikipedia, and compare it to the results achieved by the presented methods.

1 Introduction

Cross-referencing documents is an essential part of organising textual information. However, keeping links in large, quickly growing, document collections up-to-date, is problematic due to the number of possible connections. In multilingual document collections, interlinking semantically related information in a timely manner becomes even more challenging. Suitable software tools that could facilitate the link discovery process by automatically analysing the multilingual content are currently lacking. In this paper, we present new methods for Cross-Lingual Link Discovery (CLLD) applicable across different types of multilingual textual collections.

Our methods are based on Explicit Semantic Analysis (ESA) introduced by Gabrilovich and Markovitch (2007). ESA is a method that calculates semantic relatedness of two texts by mapping their term vectors to a high dimensional space (typically, but not necessarily, the space of Wikipedia concepts) and by calculating the similarity between these vectors (instead of comparing them directly). The method has received much attention in the recent years and it has also been extended to a multilingual version called Cross-Lingual Explicit Semantic Analysis (CL-ESA) (Sorg and Cimiano, 2008). To the best of our knowledge, this method has not yet been applied in the context of automatic link discovery systems.

Since the CLLD field is relatively young, it is also important to establish a constructive means for evaluating these systems. Our paper provides insight into this problem by investigating the agreement/reliability of man-made links and by presenting a possible approach for the definition of ground truth, i.e. gold standard.

The paper brings the following contributions:

(a) It applies Explicit Semantic Analysis to the link discovery and CLLD tasks.

(b) It provides new insights into the evaluation of CLLD systems and into the way people link information in different languages, as measured by their agreement.

2 Related Work

CLLD Methods

Current approaches to link detection can be divided into three groups:

(1) *link-based* approaches discover new links by exploiting an existing link graph (Itakura and Clarke, 2008; Jenkinson et al., 2008; Lu et al., 2008).

(2) *semi-structured* approaches try to discover new links using semi-structured information, such as the anchor texts or document titles (Geva, 2007; Dopichaj et al., 2008; Granitzer et al., 2008; Milne and Witten, 2008; Mihalcea and Csomai, 2007).

Proceedings of the 5th International Joint Conference on Natural Language Processing, pages 2–10,
Chiang Mai, Thailand, November 8-12, 2011.

(3) *purely content-based* approaches use as an input plain text only. They typically discover related resources by calculating semantic similarity based on document vectors (Allan, 1997; Green, 1998; Zeng and Bloniarz, 2004; Zhang and Kamps, 2008; He, 2008). Some of the mentioned approaches, such as (Lu et al., 2008), combine multiple approaches. To the best of our knowledge, no approach has so far been reported to use Explicit Semantic Analysis to address this task.

The main disadvantage of the link-based and semi-structured approaches is probably the difficulty associated with porting them across different types of document collections. The two well-known solutions to monolingual link detection, the Geva's and Itakura's algorithms (Trotman et al., 2009), fit in these two categories. While these algorithms have been demonstrated to be effective on a specific Wikipedia set, their performance has significantly decreased when they were applied to a slightly different task of interlinking two encyclopedia collections. Purely content-based methods have been mostly found to produce slightly worse results than the two previous classes of methods, however their advantage is that their performance should remain stable across different document collections. As a result, they can always be used as part of any link discovery system and can even be combined with domain specific methods that make use of the link graph or semi-structured information. In practice, domain-specific link discovery systems can achieve high precision and recall. For example, *Wikify!* (Mihalcea and Csomai, 2007) and the link detector presented by Milne and Witten (2008) can be used to identify suitable anchors in text and enrich it with links to Wikipedia by combining multiple approaches with domain knowledge.

In this paper, we present four methods (three purely content-based and one combining the link-based and content-based approach) for CLLD based on CL-ESA. Measuring semantic similarity using ESA has been previously shown to produce better results than calculating it directly on document vectors using cosine and other similarity measures and it has also been found to outperform the results that can be obtained by measuring similarity on vectors produced by Latent Semantic Analysis (LSA) (Gabrilovich and Markovitch, 2007). Therefore, the cross-lingual extension of ESA seems a plausible choice.

Evaluation of link discovery systems

The evaluation of link discovery systems is currently problematic as there is no widely accepted gold standard. Manual development of such a standard would be costly, because: (a) the number of possible links is very high even for small collections, (b) the link generation task is subjective (Ellis et al., 1994) and (c) it is not entirely clear how the link generation task should be defined in terms of link granularity (for example, document-to-document links, anchor-to-document links, anchor-to-passage links etc.). Developing such a CLLD corpora manually would be even more complicated.

As a result, Wikipedia links were extracted and taken as the gold standard (ground truth) in a comparative evaluation in (Huang et al., 2008). The authors admit that Wikipedia links are not perfect (validity of existing links is sometimes questionable and useful links may be missing) the comparative evaluation of methods and systems should be considered informative only. For example, it would be naïve to expect that measuring *precision/recall* characteristics would be accurate.

In this paper we discuss the issues in automatically defining the ground truth for CLLD systems. We take into account the differences in the way people link content in different languages to assess the agreement between the different language versions with the goal to find out how well our system performs. Our experiments are conducted on the Wikipedia dataset, however we use the articles only as a set of documents abstracting from the Wikipedia encyclopedic nature.

3 The CLLD methods

This section describes the methods used in our experiments. The whole process of cross-language link detection is shown in Figure 1. The method takes as an input a new "orphan" document (i.e. a document that is not linked to other documents) written in the source language and automatically generates a ranked list of documents written in the target language (the suitable link targets from the source document). The task involves two steps: the *cross-language* step and the *link generation* step. We have experimented with four different CLLD methods: *CL-ESA2Links*, *CL-ESADirect*, *CL-ESA2ESA* and *CL-ESA2Similar* that will be described later on. The names of the methods

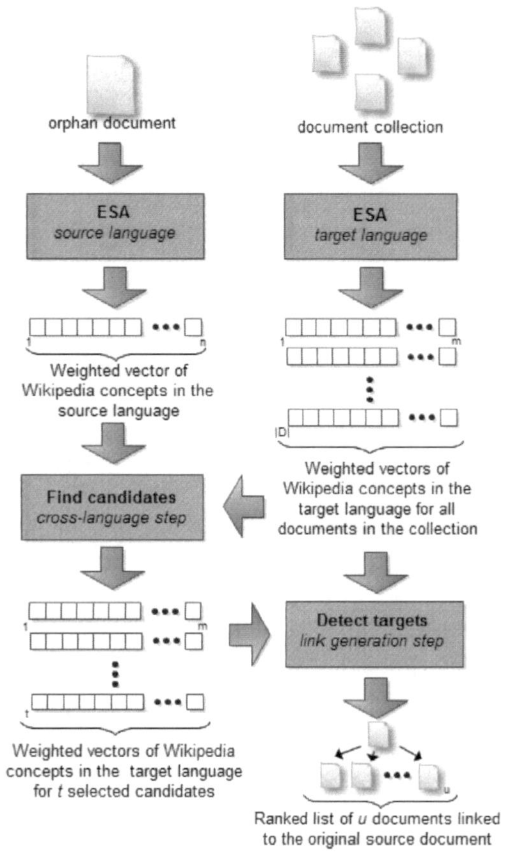

Figure 1: Cross-language link discovery process

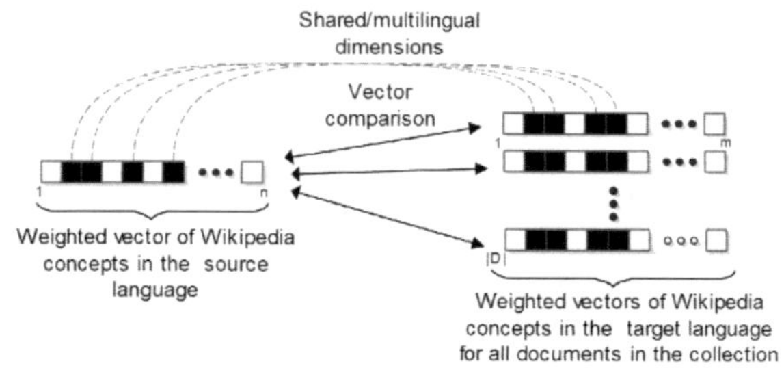

Figure 2: CLLD candidates

are derived from the approach applied in the first and the second step. These methods have different characteristics and would be useful in different scenarios.

In the **first step**, an ESA vector is calculated for each document in the document collection. This results in obtaining a weighted vector of Wikipedia concepts for each document in the target language. The cardinality of the vector is given by the number of concepts (pages) in the target language version of Wikipedia (i.e. it is about 3.8 million for English, 764,000 for Spanish, etc.). A similar procedure is applied on the orphan document, however, the source language version of ESA is used. The resulting ESA vector is then compared to the ESA vectors that represent documents in the target language collection (CL-ESA approach). A set of candidate vectors representing documents in the target language is acquired as an output of the cross-language step, see Section 3.1.

In the **second step**, the candidate vectors are taken as a seed and are used to discover documents that are suitable link targets. The four different approaches used in this step distinguish the above-mentioned methods, see Section 3.2.

3.1 The cross-language step

The main rationale for the cross-language step is to find t suitable candidates in the target language that can later be exploited to identify link targets. Semantically similar target language documents to the source language document are considered by our methods as suitable candidates. To identify such documents, the ESA vector of the source document is compared to the ESA vectors of documents in the target document collection.

Each dimension in an ESA vector expresses the similarity of a document to the given language version of a Wikipedia concept/article. Therefore, the cardinality of the source document vector is different from the cardinality of the vectors representing the documents in the target language collection (Figure 2). In order to calculate the similarity of two vectors, we map the dimensions that correspond to the same Wikipedia concepts in different language versions. In most cases, if a Wikipedia concept is mapped to another language version, there is a one-to-one correspondence between the articles in those two languages. However, there are cases when one page in the source language is mapped to more than one page in the target language and vice versa.[1] For the purpose of similarity calculation, we use 100 dimensions with the highest weight that are mappable from the source to the target language. The number of candidates to be extracted is controlled by parameter t. We have experimentally found that its selection has a significant impact on the performance of our methods.

[1]These multiple mappings appear quite rarely, e.g. in 5,889 cases out of 550,134 for Spanish to English and for 2,528 cases out of 163,715 for Czech to English.

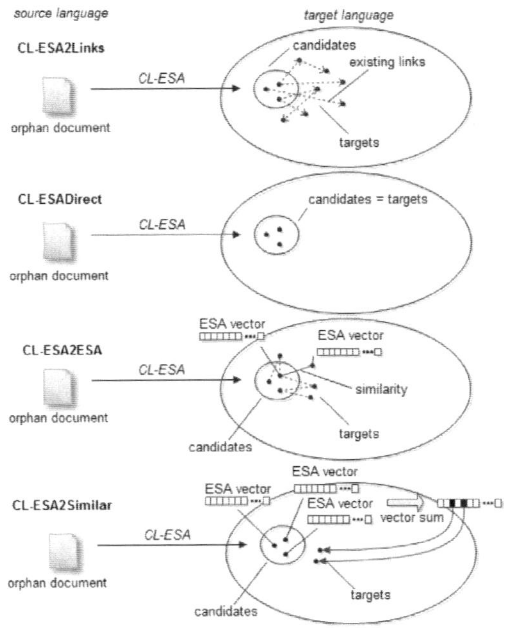

Figure 3: Schematic illustration of the four approaches used by the CLLD methods.

3.2 The link generation step

In the link generation step, the candidate documents are taken and used to produce a ranked list of targets for the original source document. The following approaches, schematically illustrated in Figure 3, are taken by our four methods:

- **CL-ESA2Links** - This method requires access to the link structure in the target collection. More precisely, the method takes the original orphan document in the source language and tries to link it to an already interlinked target language collection. After applying CL-ESA in the first step, existing links are extracted from the candidate documents. The link targets are then ranked according to their similarity to the source document, i.e. documents that are more similar are ranked higher. This list is then used as a collection of link targets.

- **CL-ESADirect** - This method applies CL-ESA on the source document and takes the list of candidates directly as link targets.

- **CL-ESA2ESA** - In this method, the application of CL-ESA is followed by another application of monolingual ESA, which measures the semantic similarity of the candidates with all documents in the document collection, to identify link targets.

- **CL-ESA2Similar** - Instead of generating the ranked list of link targets using monolingual ESA as in the previous method, which is computationally expensive, we calculate a vector sum from the candidate list of ESA document vectors. We then select strong Wiki concepts representing these dimensions as the set of targets. This is equivalent to calculating cosine similarity using *tfidf* vectors. Though much quicker, the main disadvantage is that if we wanted to use this method on another set than Wikipedia, ESA would have to be used with a different background collection.

All of the methods have different properties. CL-ESA2Links requires the knowledge of the link graph in the target document collection. CL-ESA2ESA and ESADirect are two methods that are universal, i.e. can be easily applied in any document collection. The difference between them is that the former one requires significantly less document vector comparisons than the later method. CL-ESA2Similar works almost as fast as CL-ESADirect, but it has the disadvantage that ESA has to be used with the specific document collection as a background.

4 The underlying data

Wikipedia has been used as a corpus for the methods evaluation. This decision has the following advantages that make it possible for us to test and analyse the methods on a real use case:

- A very large multilingual text collection.
- The articles are well-interlinked and the interlinking has been approved by a large community of users.
- A large proportion of articles contain explicit mapping between different language versions.

In our study, we have experimented with the English, Spanish and Czech language versions of Wikipedia. We consider the cases of linking from Spanish to English and from Czech to English, i.e. from a less resourced language to the more resourced one. We believe that this is the more interesting direction for CLLD methods as the target language version is more likely to contain relevant information not available in the source language. The language selection has been motivated by the aim to test the methods in two very different environments. The Spanish version is relatively well resourced containing 764,095 pages (about four times fewer than English), the Czech language is much less resourced containing 196,494 pages (about four times fewer than Spanish).

5 Evaluation methodology

One of the main obstacles in systematically improving link discovery systems is the difficulty to evaluate the results. The issue that makes reliable evaluation problematic is due to both technical and cognitive aspects. The difficulty in obtaining the "ground truth" for a sufficiently large dataset is caused both by the lack of human resources to manually annotate a very large number of document combinations, and the inherent subjectivity of the task. As a result, we find it essential to estimate the agreement between annotators and see to what extent the precision and recall characteristics can be measured with respect to interlinked document collections.

We claim that the reasons for linking two pieces of information is made at the level of semantics, i.e. the annotator has to understand the concepts/ideas described in two papers to decide if they should be connected by a link. We claim that this process should be language independent. Thus, an article about London will be related to an article about the United Kingdom regardless of the language the articles are written in.

Therefore, let us define the link generation task in the following way: Given a document[2] in the source language, find documents in the target language that are suitable link targets for the source document, i.e. there is a semantic relationship between the source document and the linked target documents.

Based on the definition, the ground truth for a topic document d is the set of documents that can be considered (semantically) suitable link targets. Though this set is typically unknown to us, we can in our experiment approximate it by taking the existing Wikipedia links as ground truth. Because the Wikipedia link structure has been agreed by a large number of contributing authors, it is likely to have a relatively consistent link structure in comparison to content that would be linked just by a single person. To establish the ground truth for the original source document, we can extract all links originating in the source document and pointing to other documents. Since the process of linking information is performed at the semantic level, and is thus language independent, we can enrich our ground truth with link graphs from different language versions of Wikipedia. This causes the ground truth to get larger which has two consequences: (1) It increases the reliability of the evaluation as many relevant links are often omitted (Knoth et al., 2010) (2) It is more difficult to achieve higher recall.

6 Results

6.1 Experimental setup

The experiment was carried out for two language pairs: Spanish to English and Czech to English. We will denote the source language L_{source} and the target language L_{target}. The input for the different CLLD methods are two document sets:

- Let $SOURCE_{L_{source}}$ be the set of topic documents selected as pages that contain a Wikipedia link between different language versions. In our case, 100 pages were selected.
- Let $TARGET_{L_{target}}$ be the collection of documents in the target language from which the link targets are selected. In our case, this collection contains all (3.8 million) Wikipedia pages in English.

The output of the method is a set (ranked list) $LIST_{result} = \langle TARGET_{L_{target}}, score \rangle$. To establish the ground truth we define:

- Let ρ be the mapping from documents in the source language to their target language versions $\rho : D_{L_{source}} \rightarrow D_{L_{target}}$.
- Let $SOURCE_{L_{target}}$ be the set of topic documents mapped to the target language $SOURCE_{L_{target}} = \rho SOURCE_{L_{source}}$.
- Let α, β be the mappings from documents to the other documents they link to in the source and target language respectively $\alpha : D_{L_{source}} \rightarrow D_{L_{source}}$, $\beta : D_{L_{target}} \rightarrow D_{L_{target}}$.

[2]The term *topic* is also sometimes used to refer to the document.

then we define the ground truth (GT) as the union of ground truths for different language versions, in this experiment we define it as the union of ground truth for the source and target language.

$$GT = \alpha(SOURCE_{L_{source}}) \cup \beta(SOURCE_{L_{target}})$$

A given generated item $\langle d, score \rangle \in LIST_{result}$ is evaluated as a hit if and only if $d \in GT$.

6.2 Methods evaluation

To investigate the performance of the first part of CLLD - the cross-language step carried out by CL-ESA, we have analysed how well the system finds for a given topic document in the source language the duplicate document in the target language. In this step, the system takes a document in the source language, and selects from the 3.8 million large document set in the target language the documents with the highest similarity. We then check, if a duplicate document ($d = \rho d_{source}$) appears among the top k retrieved documents. The experiment is repeated for all examples in $SOURCE_{L_{source}}$ and the results are then averaged (Figure 4). The graph suggests that the method performs well, as the document often appears among the first few results. In about 65% of cases, the document is found among the first 50 retrieved items. We believe that if the set of candidates (controlled by the t parameter) contains this document, the CLLD method is likely to produce better results, this is especially true for the CL-ESA2Links method.

The overall results for all the methods are presented in Figure 5. We have experimentally set $t = 10$ for Spanish to English and $t = 3$ for Czech to English CLLD. CL-ESA2Links performed in the experiments the best achieving 0.2 precision at 0.3 recall. CL-ESA2Similar performed the best out of the purely content-based methods.

Though the precision/recall might seem quite low, a number of things should be taken into account:

- A significant number of potentially useful links is still missing in our ground truth, because people typically do not intend to link all relevant information. As a result, many potentially useful connections are not explicitly present in Wikipedia (Knoth et al., 2010).

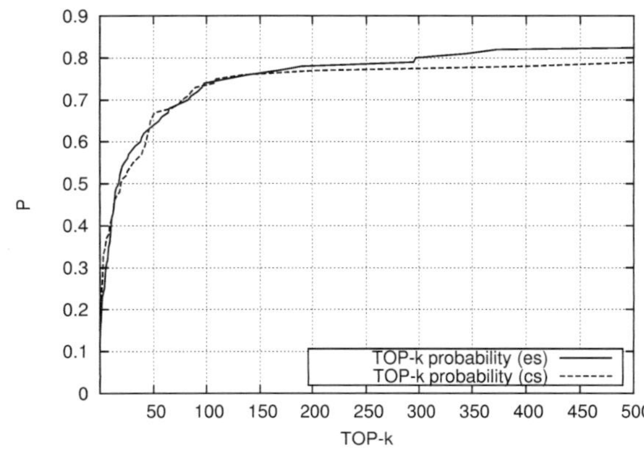

Figure 4: The probability (y-axis) of finding the target language version of a given source language document using CL-ESA in the top k retrieved documents (x-axis). Drawn as a cumulative distribution function.

  The problem can be partly mitigated by combining the ground truth from more language versions. Another approach is to measure the agreement instead of precision/recall characteristics (see Section 6.3).

- A significant number of links in Wikipedia are conceptual links. These links do not express a particularly strong relationship at the article level. This makes it very difficult for the pure-content based methods to find them, which results in low recall. It seems that CL-ESA2Links is the only method that does not suffer from this issue.

- The experiment settings make it hard for the methods to achieve high precision/recall performance. The $TARGET_{L_{target}}$ set contains 3.8 million articles, out of which, the methods are supposed to identify on average just a small subset of target documents. More precisely, in Spanish to English CLLD, our ground truth contains on average 341 target documents with standard deviation 293, in Czech to English, it contains on average 382 target documents with standard deviation 292.

6.3 Measuring the agreement

To assess the subjectivity of the link generation task and to investigate the reliability of the acquired ground truth, we have compared the link structures from different language version of

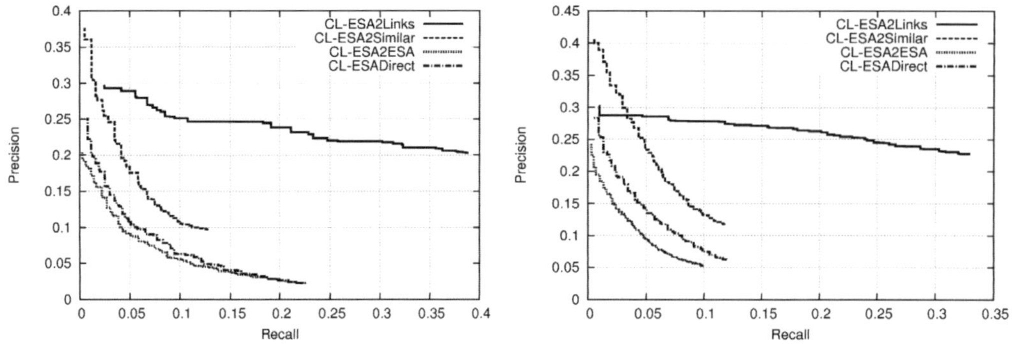

Figure 5: The precision ($y - axis$)/recall (x-axis) graphs for Spanish to English (left) and Czech to English (right) CLLD methods.

Spanish vs English			
	Y_{en}	N_{en}	N/A_{en}
Y_{es}	5,563	10,201	3,934
N_{es}	15,715	539,299,641	99,191,766
N/A_{es}	5781	321,326,145	0
Czech vs English			
	Y_{en}	N_{en}	N/A_{en}
Y_{cz}	4,308	8,738	2,194
N_{cz}	12,961	392,411,445	7,501,806
N/A_{cz}	9,790	356,532,740	0

Table 1: The agreement of Spanish and English Wikipedia and Czech and English Wikipedia on their link structures calculated and summed for all pages in $SOURCE_{es}$. Y - indicates yes, N - no, N/A - not available/no decision

Wikipedia. We have iterated over the set of topics from $SOURCE_{L_{source}}$ and recorded for each document in $TARGET_{L_{target}}$ in each step if it is a valid link target (yes - Y) or if it is not a valid link target (no - N) for the given source document in each language, thus measuring the agreement between the link structures in different languages. The results are presented in Table 1.

As demonstrated in Figure 6, a subset of Wikipedia pages cannot be mapped to other language versions. Either the semantically equivalent page does not exist or the cross-language link is missing. These links were classified as no decision/not available (N/A). The mappable documents were classified in a standard way according to their appearance in the link graphs of the language versions. Only these links are taken into account while measuring the agreement.

A common way to assess inter-annotator agreement between two raters in Information Retrieval is using the Cohen's Kappa calculated as:

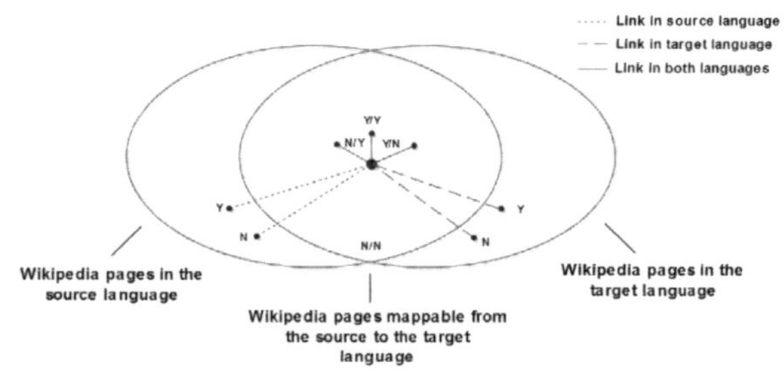

Figure 6: Individual cases of agreement/disagreement/no decision (not available) for two language versions of Wikipedia link graphs.

$$\kappa = \frac{Pr(a) - Pr(e)}{1 - Pr(e)},$$

where $Pr(a)$ is the relative observed frequency of agreement and $Pr(e)$ is the hypothetical probability of chance agreement. $Pr(a)$ is typically calculated as $\frac{|Y,Y|+|N,N|}{|Y,Y|+|Y,N|+|N,Y|+|N,N|}$. Since there is a strong agreement on the negative decisions, the probability will be close to 1. If we ignore the $|N,N|$ cases, which do not carry any useful information, the formula looks as follows:

$$Pr(a) = \frac{|Y,Y|}{|Y,Y| + |Y,N| + |N,Y|}.$$

The probability of a random agreement is extremely low, because the probability of a link

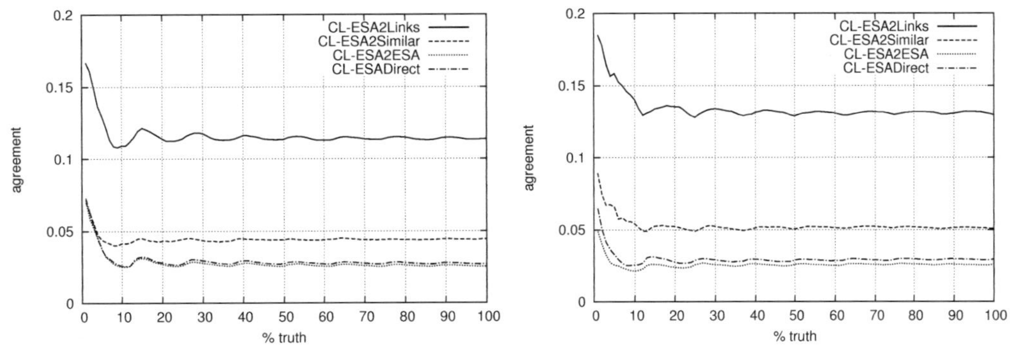

Figure 7: The agreements of the Spanish to English (left) and Czech to English (right) CLLD methods with $GT_{es,en}$ and $GT_{cz,en}$ respectively. The y-axis shows the agreement strength and the x-axis the number of generated examples as a fraction of the number of examples in ground truth.

connecting any two pages is approximately:[3]

$$p_{link} = \frac{|links|}{|pages|^2} = \frac{78.3M}{3.2M^2} = 0.000007648.$$

Thus, the hypothetical number of items appearing in the Y, Y class by chance is $p^2_{link} \cdot (|Y, Y| + |Y, N| + |N, Y| + |N, N|)$. This formula estimates the number of agreements achieved by chance. In our case the value is much smaller than 1, hence $P(e)$ is close to 0. Therefore, we can calculate the agreement for English and Spanish as:

$$\kappa_{en,es} = \frac{5,563}{31,479} = 0.177.$$

The agreement for Czech and English is:

$$\kappa_{en,cz} = \frac{4,308}{26,007} = 0.166.$$

The value indicates a relatively low inter-annotator agreement. We believe that the fact that such a low agreement has been measured is very interesting, particularly because the link structure in Wikipedia is a result of a collaborative effort of many contributors. Therefore, we would expect that even lower agreement might be experienced in other types of text collections.

Motivated by the previous findings, we have calculated the agreement between the output of our method and the link graphs present in different language versions of Wikipedia. We were especially interested to find out if the agreement is significantly different from the agreement measured between different language versions of Wikipedia. We have generated by our CLLD methods 100% of $|GT|$ links for every orphan document in $SOURCE_{L_{source}}$, i.e. if a particular document is linked in Wikipedia to 57 documents, we generate 57 links. We have then measured the agreement for each topic document and averaged the agreement values. The results of the experiment for Spanish to English and Czech to English CLLD are shown in Figure 7. They suggest that CL-ESA2Links achieved a level of agreement comparable to that of human annotators. A very reasonable level of agreement has also been measured for CL-ESA2Similar, especially for the first 10% of the generated links. CL-ESADirect and CL-ESA2ESA exhibit a lower level of agreement.

7 Conclusion

In this paper, we have presented and evaluated four different methods for Cross-Language Link Discovery (CLLD). We have used Cross-language Explicit Semantic Analysis as a key component in the development of the four presented methods. The results suggest that methods that are aware of the link graph in the target language achieve slightly better results than those that identify links in the target language only by calculating semantic similarity. However, the former methods cannot be applied in all document collections and thus the later methods are valuable. Though it might seem at first sight that CLLD methods do not provide very high precision and recall, we have shown that the performance can, in fact, reach the results achieved by human annotators.

[3]Following the official Wikipedia statistics. Though different language versions have different p_{link}, the differences do not effect the results.

References

James Allan. 1997. Building hypertext using information retrieval. *Inf. Process. Manage.*, 33:145–159, March.

Philipp Dopichaj, Andre Skusa, and Andreas Heß. 2008. Stealing anchors to link the wiki. In Geva et al. (Geva et al., 2009), pages 343–353.

David Ellis, Jonathan Furner-Hines, and Peter Willett. 1994. On the measurement of inter-linker consistency and retrieval effectiveness in hypertext databases. In *SIGIR '94: Proceedings of the 17th annual international ACM SIGIR conference on Research and development in information retrieval*, pages 51–60, New York, NY, USA. Springer-Verlag New York, Inc.

Evgeniy Gabrilovich and Shaul Markovitch. 2007. Computing semantic relatedness using wikipedia-based explicit semantic analysis. In *In Proceedings of the 20th International Joint Conference on Artificial Intelligence*, pages 1606–1611.

Shlomo Geva, Jaap Kamps, and Andrew Trotman, editors. 2009. *Advances in Focused Retrieval, 7th International Workshop of the Initiative for the Evaluation of XML Retrieval, INEX 2008, Dagstuhl Castle, Germany, December 15-18, 2008. Revised and Selected Papers*, Lecture Notes in Computer Science. Springer.

Shlomo Geva. 2007. Gpx: Ad-hoc queries and automated link discovery in the wikipedia. In Norbert Fuhr, Jaap Kamps, Mounia Lalmas, and Andrew Trotman, editors, *INEX*, Lecture Notes in Computer Science. Springer.

Michael Granitzer, Christin Seifert, and Mario Zechner. 2008. Context based wikipedia linking. In Geva et al. (Geva et al., 2009), pages 354–365.

Stephen J. Green. 1998. Automated link generation: can we do better than term repetition? *Comput. Netw. ISDN Syst.*, 30(1-7):75–84.

Jiyin He. 2008. Link detection with wikipedia. In Geva et al. (Geva et al., 2009), pages 366–373.

Wei Che Huang, Andrew Trotman, and Shlomo Geva. 2008. Experiments and evaluation of link discovery in the wikipedia.

Kelly Y. Itakura and Charles L. A. Clarke. 2008. University of waterloo at inex 2008: Adhoc, book, and link-the-wiki tracks. In Geva et al. (Geva et al., 2009), pages 132–139.

Dylan Jenkinson, Kai-Cheung Leung, and Andrew Trotman. 2008. Wikisearching and wikilinking. In Geva et al. (Geva et al., 2009), pages 374–388.

Petr Knoth, Jakub Novotny, and Zdenek Zdrahal. 2010. Automatic generation of inter-passage links based on semantic similarity. In *Proceedings of the 23rd International Conference on Computational Linguistics (Coling 2010)*, pages 590–598, Beijing, China, August.

Wei Lu, Dan Liu, and Zhenzhen Fu. 2008. Csir at inex 2008 link-the-wiki track. In Geva et al. (Geva et al., 2009), pages 389–394.

Rada Mihalcea and Andras Csomai. 2007. Wikify!: linking documents to encyclopedic knowledge. In *Proceedings of the sixteenth ACM conference on Conference on information and knowledge management*, CIKM '07, pages 233–242, New York, NY, USA. ACM.

David Milne and Ian H. Witten. 2008. Learning to link with wikipedia. In James G. Shanahan, Sihem Amer-Yahia, Ioana Manolescu, Yi Zhang, David A. Evans, Aleksander Kolcz, Key-Sun Choi, and Abdur Chowdhury, editors, *CIKM*, pages 509–518. ACM.

Philipp Sorg and Philipp Cimiano. 2008. Cross-lingual information retrieval with explicit semantic analysis. In *Working Notes for the CLEF 2008 Workshop*.

Andrew Trotman, David Alexander, and Shlomo Geva. 2009. Overview of the inex 2010 link the wiki track.

Jihong Zeng and Peter A. Bloniarz. 2004. From keywords to links: an automatic approach. *Information Technology: Coding and Computing, International Conference on*, 1:283.

Junte Zhang and Jaap Kamps. 2008. A content-based link detection approach using the vector space model. In Geva et al. (Geva et al., 2009), pages 395–400.

Cross Language POS Taggers (and other Tools) for Indian Languages: An Experiment with Kannada using Telugu Resources

Siva Reddy
Lexical Computing Ltd, UK
siva@sketchengine.co.uk

Serge Sharoff
University of Leeds, UK
s.sharoff@leeds.ac.uk

Abstract

Indian languages are known to have a large speaker base, yet some of these languages have minimal or non-efficient linguistic resources. For example, Kannada is relatively resource-poor compared to Malayalam, Tamil and Telugu, which in-turn are relatively poor compared to Hindi. Many Indian language pairs exhibit high similarities in morphology and syntactic behaviour e.g. Kannada is highly similar to Telugu. In this paper, we show how to build a cross-language part-of-speech tagger for Kannada exploiting the resources of Telugu. We also build large corpora and a morphological analyser (including lemmatisation) for Kannada. Our experiments reveal that a cross-language taggers are as efficient as mono-lingual taggers. We aim to extend our work to other Indian languages. Our tools are efficient and significantly faster than the existing mono-lingual tools.

1 Introduction

Part-of-speech (POS) taggers are some of the basic tools for natural language processing in any language. For example, they are needed for terminology extraction using linguistic patterns or for selecting word lists in language teaching and lexicography. At the same time, many languages lack POS taggers. One reasons for this is the lack of other basic resources like corpora, lexicons or morphological analysers. With the advent of Web, collecting corpora is no longer a major problem (Kilgarriff et al., 2010). With technical advances in lexicography (Atkins and Rundell, 2008), building lexicons and morphological analysers is also possible to considerable extent.

The other reason for the lack of POS taggers is partly due the lack of researchers working on a particular language. Due to this, some languages do not have any annotated data to build efficient taggers.

Cross-language research mainly aims to build tools for a resource-poor language (target language) using the resources of a resource-rich language (source language). If the target language is typologically related to the source one, it is possible to rely on the resource rich language.

In this work, we aim to find if cross language tools for Indian languages are any efficient as compared to existing mono-lingual tools. As a use case, we experiment with the resource-poor language Kannada, by building various cross-language POS taggers, using the resources of its typologically-related and relatively resource-rich language Telugu. Our POS taggers can also be used as a morphological analyser since our POS tags include morphological information. We also build a lemmatiser for Kannada which uses POS tag information to choose a relevant lemma from the set of plausible lemmas.

2 Related Work

There are several methods for building POS taggers for a target language using source language resources. Some researchers (Yarowsky et al., 2001; Yarowsky and Ngai, 2001; Das and Petrov, 2011) built POS taggers for a target language using parallel corpus. The source (cross) language is expected to have a POS tagger. First, the source language tools annotate the source side of the parallel corpora. Later these annotations are projected to the target language side using the alignments in the parallel corpora, creating virtual annotated corpora for the target language. A POS tagger for the target is then built from the virtual annotated corpora. Other methods which make use of parallel corpora are (Snyder et al., 2008; Naseem et al., 2009). These approaches are based on hierarchical Bayesian models and Markov Chain Monte Carlo

Proceedings of the 5th International Joint Conference on Natural Language Processing, pages 11–19,
Chiang Mai, Thailand, November 8-12, 2011.

sampling techniques. They aim to gain from information shared across languages. The main disadvantage of all such methods is that they rely on parallel corpora which itself is a costly resource for resource-poor languages.

Hana et al. (2004) and Feldman et al. (2006) propose a method for developing a POS tagger for a target language using the resources of another typologically related language. Our method is motivated from them, but with the focus on resources available for Indian languages.

2.1 Hana et al. (2004)

Hana et al. aim to develop a tagger for Russian from Czech using TnT (Brants, 2000), a second-order Markov model. Though the languages Czech and Russian are free-word order, they argue that TnT is as efficient as other models.

TnT tagger is based on two probabilities - the transition and emission probabilities. The tag sequence of a given word sequence is selected by calculating

$$\underset{t_1 \ldots t_n}{\operatorname{argmax}} \left[\prod_{i=1}^{n} P(t_i|t_{i-1}, t_{i-2}) P(w_i|t_i) \right] \quad (1)$$

where $w_i \ldots w_n$ is the word sequence and $t_1 \ldots t_n$ are their corresponding POS tags.

Transition probabilities, $P(t_i|t_{i-1}, t_{i-2})$, describe the conditional probability of a tag given the tags of previous words. Based on the intuition that transition probabilities across typologically related languages remain the same, Hana et al. treat the transition probabilities of Russian to be the same as Czech.

Emission probabilities, $P(w_i|t_i)$, describe the conditional probability of a word given a tag. It is not straightforward to estimate emission probabilities from a cross-language. Instead, Hana et al. develop a light paradigm-based (a set of rules) lexicon for Russian which emits all the possible tags for a given word form. The distribution of all the tags of a word is treated to be uniform. Using this assumption, surrogate emission probabilities of Russian are estimated without using Czech.

The accuracy of the cross-pos tagger, i.e. the tagger of Russian built using Czech, is found to be encouraging.

2.2 Existing Tools for Kannada

There exists literature on Kannada morphological analysers (Vikram and Urs, 2007; Antony et al., 2010; Shambhavi et al., 2011) and POS taggers (Antony and Soman, 2010) but none of them have any publicly downloadable resources. Murthy (2000) gives an overview of existing resources for Kannada and points out that most of these exist without public access. We are interested only in the work whose tools are publicly available for download.

We found only one downloadable POS tagger for Kannada developed by the Indian Language Machine Translation (ILMT) consortium[1]. The consortium publicly released tools for 9 Indian languages including Kannada and Telugu. The available tools are transliterators, morphological analysers, POS taggers and shallow parsers.

The POS taggers from the ILMT consortium are mono-lingual POS taggers i.e. trained using the target language resources itself. These were developed by Avinesh and Karthik (2007) by training a conditional random fields (CRF) model on the training data provided by the participating institutions in the consortium. In the public evaluation of POS taggers for Indian languages (Bharati and Mannem, 2007), the tagger (Avinesh and Karthik, 2007) was ranked best among all the existing taggers.

Indian languages are morphologically rich with Dravidian languages posing extra challenge because of their agglutinative nature. Avinesh and Karthik (2007) noted that morphological information play an important role in Indian language POS tagging. Their CRF model is trained on all the important morphological features to predict the output tag for a word in a given context. The pipeline of (Avinesh and Karthik, 2007) can be described as below

1. Tokenise the Unicode input
2. Transliterate the tokenised input to ASCII format.
3. Run the morph analyser to get all the morphological sets possible
4. Extract relevant morphological features used by the CRF model
5. Given a word, based on the morphological features of its context and itself, the CRF

[1]Tools for 9 Indian languages http://ltrc.iiit.ac.in/showfile.php?filename=downloads/shallow_parser.php

Field	Description	Number of Tags	Tags
	Full Tag	311	NN.n.f.pl.3.d, VM.v.n.sg.3., ...
1	Main POS Tag	25	CC, JJ, NN, VM, ...
2	Coarse POS Category	9	adj, n, num, unk ...
3	Gender	6	any, f, m, n, punc, null
4	Number	4	any, pl, sg, null
5	Person	5	1, 2, 3, any, null
6	Case	3	d, o, null

Table 1: Fields in each tag and its corresponding statistics. *null* denotes empty value, e.g. in the tag *VM.v.n..3.*, *number* and *case* fields are *null*

model annotate the word with a relevant POS tag

6. Transliterate the ASCII output to Unicode

The major drawback with this tagging model is that it relies on a pipeline and if something breaks in the pipeline, the POS tagger doesn't work. We found that the tagger annotates only 78% of the input sentences. The tagger is found to be too slow to scale for large annotation tasks.

We aim to remove this pipeline, yet build an efficient tagger which also performs morphological analysis at the same time.

2.3 Kannada and Telugu Background

Kannada and Telugu are spoken by 35 and 75 million people respectively[2]. Majority of the existing research in Indian languages focused on few languages like Hindi, Marathi, Bengali, Telugu and Tamil, as a result of which other languages like Kannada, Malayalam are relatively resource-poor.

Telugu is known to be highly influenced by Kannada, making the languages slightly mutually intelligible (Datta, 1998, pg. 1690). Until 13th century both the languages have same script. In the later years, the script has changed but still close similarities can be observed. Both the scripts belong to the same script family.

The similarities between Kannada and Telugu, and the relative resource abundance in Telugu, motivates us to develop a cross language POS tagger for Kannada using Telugu.

3 Our Tagset

All the Indian languages have similarities in morphological properties and syntactic behaviour. The only main difference is the agglutinative behaviour of Dravidian languages. Observing these similarities and differences in Indian languages, Bharati et al. (2006) proposed a common POS tagset for all Indian languages. Avinesh and Karthik (2007) use this tagset.

We encode morphological information to the above tagset creating a *fine-grained POS tagset* similar to the work of (Schmid and Laws, 2008) for German, which is morphologically rich like Kannada. Each tag consists of 6 fields. Table 1 describe each field and its statistics. For example, our tag **NN.n.m.sg.3.o** represents the main POS tag 'NN' for *common noun* as defined by (Bharati et al., 2006), 'n' for coarse grained category *noun*, 'm' for *masculine* gender, 'sg' for *singular* number, '3' for 3rd *person*, 'o' for *oblique* case. For more guidelines on morphological labels, please refer to (Bharati et al., 2007).

Since our POS tag encodes morphological information in itself, our tagger could also be used as a morphological analyser. A sample sentence POS tagged by our tagger is displayed in Figure 1.

4 Our Method

We aim to build a Hidden-Markov model (HMM) based Kannada POS tagger described by the Equation 1. We use TnT (Brants, 2000), a popular implementation of the second-order Markov model for POS tagging. We construct the TnT model by estimating transition and emission probabilities of Kannada using the cross-language Telugu. Since our tagset has both POS and morphological information encoded in it, the HMM model has an advantage of using morphological information to predict the main POS tag, and the inverse, where main POS tag helps to predict the morphological information. Briefly, the steps involved in our method are

1. Download large corpora of Kannada and Telugu

[2]Source: Wikipedia

Word	POS Tag	Lemma.Suffix
ಕತೆಯ	NN.n.n.sg..o	ಕತೆ.ಅ
ಪ್ರಕಾರ	NN.n.n.sg..d	ಪ್ರಕಾರ.0
ಗೆಳೆಯರೊಂದಿಗಿನ	NN.unk....	ಗೆಳೆಯರೊಂದಿಗಿನ.
ಆಟದಲ್ಲಿ	NN.n.n.sg..o	ಆಟ.ಅಲ್ಲಿ
ರಾಜನಾಗಿದ್ದ	VM.unk....	ರಾಜನಾಗಿದ್ದ.
ಚಂದ್ರಗುಪ್ತನು	NNP.unk....	ಚಂದ್ರಗುಪ್ತನು.
ಅಪರಾಧಿಯ	NN.n.m.sg.3.o	ಅಪರಾಧಿ.ಅ
ಪಾತ್ರ	NN.n.n.sg..d	ಪಾತ್ರ.0
ವಹಿಸಿದ್ದ	VM.v.any.any.any.	ವಹಿಸು.ಇದ್ದ
ಇನ್ನೊಬ್ಬ	QC.unk....	ಇನ್ನೊಬ್ಬ.
ಹುಡುಗನ	NN.n.m.sg.3.o	ಹುಡುಗ.ಅ
ವಿಚಾರಣೆಯನ್ನು	NN.n.n.sg..o	ವಿಚಾರಣೆ.ಅನ್ನು
ಮಾಡಿ	VM.v..pl.2.	ಮಾಡು.0
ಶಿಕ್ಷೆ	NN.n.n.sg..d	ಶಿಕ್ಷೆ.0
ವಿಧಿಸುತ್ತಿದ್ದನು	VM.v.m.sg.3.	ವಿಧಿಸು.ಉತ್ತಿದ್
.	SYM.punc....	..

Figure 1: A Sample POS Tagging and Lemmatisation for a Kannada Sentence

2. Determine the transition probabilities of Telugu by training TnT on the machine annotated corpora of Telugu. Since Telugu and Kannada are typologically related, we assume the transition probabilities of Kannada to be the same as of Telugu
3. Estimate the emission probabilities of Kannada from machine annotated Telugu corpus or machine annotate Kannada corpus
4. Use the probabilities from the step 2 and 3 to build a POS tagger for Kannada

4.1 Step1: Kannada and Telugu Corpus Creation

Corpus collection once used to be long, slow and expensive. But with the advent of the Web and the success of Web-as-Corpus notion (Kilgarriff and Grefenstette, 2003), corpus collection can be highly automated, and thereby fast and inexpensive.

We have used *Corpus Factory* method (Kilgarriff et al., 2010) to collect Kannada and Telugu corpora from the Web. The method is described in the following steps.

Frequency List: Corpus Factory method requires a frequency list of the language of interest to start corpus collection. The frequency list of the language is built from its Wikipedia dump[3]. The dump is processed to remove all the Wiki and HTML markup to extract raw corpus, the Wiki corpus. The frequency list is then built from the tokenised Wiki corpus.

Seed Word Collection: We treat the top 1000 words of the frequency list as the *high-frequency words* of the language and the next 5000 as the mid-frequency ones which we shall use as our *seed words*.

Query Generation: 30,000 random queries of 2-word size are generated such that no query is identical nor its permutations.

URL Collection: Each query is sent to Bing[4] search engine and the pages corresponding to the hits are downloaded. These pages are converted to UTF-8 encoding.

Filtering Above pages are cleaned to remove boiler-plate text (i.e. html and irrelevant blocks like ads) extracting the plain text. Some of these pages are found to be in foreign languages and some of them are found to be spam. We applied a simple language modelling based filter to remove these pages. The filter validates only the pages in

[3]Wikipedia Dumps: `http://dumps.wikimedia.org`

[4]Bing: `http://bing.com`

which the ratio of non-frequent words to the high-frequent words is maintained. If a page doesn't meet this criteria, we discard it.

Near-Duplicate Removal: The above filter isn't sufficient to discard the pages which are duplicates. In-order to detect them, we used Broder et al. (1997) near-duplicate detection algorithm, and store only one page among the duplicates.

Finally we collected cleaned corpora of 16 million words for Kannada and 4.6 million words for Telugu[5].

4.2 Step 2: Estimating Kannada Transition Probabilities

Transition probabilities represent the probability of transition to a state from the previous states. Here each state represents a tag and hence $P(t_i|t_{i-1}, t_{i-2})$. We estimate transition probabilities in two different ways.

4.2.1 From the source language

Across typologically related languages, it is likely that transition probabilities among tags are the same. We assume the transition probabilities of Telugu to be approximately equal to the transition probabilities of Kannada.

One can estimate the transition probabilities of a language from its manually annotated corpora. Since we do not have the manually annotated Telugu corpora publicly available, we have used (Avinesh and Karthik, 2007) to tag the Telugu corpus downloaded in Step 1. This tagged corpus captures an approximation of the true transition probabilities in the manually annotated corpora.

The tagged corpus is converted to the format in Figure 1 and then using TnT we estimate transition probabilities.

4.2.2 From the target language

Apart from using Telugu transition probabilities, we also experimented with the existing Kannada POS tagger. We annotated the Kannada corpus collected in Step 1 using the existing tagger. We then estimated the transition probabilities from the machine annotated Kannada corpus. Note that if Kannada POS tagger is used for estimating transition probabilities, our tagger can no longer be called a cross-language tagger, and is mono-lingual. This tagger is used to compare the performance of cross-lingual and mono-lingual taggers.

[5]Telugu is collected two years back and Kannada very recently and so are the differences in sizes.

Since we learn the transition probabilities of the fine-grained POS tags from a large corpora, this helps in building a robust and efficient tagger compared to the existing mono-lingual tagger. Robust because we would be able to predict POS and morphological information for unseen words, and efficient because the morphological information helps in better POS prediction and vice versa.

4.3 Step 3: Estimating Kannada Emission Probabilities

Emission probabilities represent the probabilities of an emission (output) of a given state. Here state corresponds to tag and emission to a word and hence $P(w_i|t_i)$. We tried various ways of estimating emission probabilities of Kannada.

4.3.1 Approximate string matching

It is not easy to estimate emission probabilities of a language from a cross language without the help of either parallel corpora or a bilingual dictionary or a translation system. Since the languages, Kannada and Telugu, are slightly mutually intelligible (Datta, 1998, pg. 1690), we aimed to exploit lexical similarities between Kannada and Telugu to the extent possible.

Firstly, a Telugu lexicon is built by training TnT on the machine annotated Telugu corpora (Step 1). The lexicon has the information of each Telugu word and its corresponding POS tags along with their frequencies. Then, a word list for Kannada is built from the Kannada corpus. For a every Kannada word, the most probable similar Telugu word is determined using approximate string matching [6]. To measure similarity, we transliterated both Kannada and Telugu words to a common ASCII encoding. For example, the most similar Telugu words of the Kannada word *xAswAnu* are ('xAswAn', 0.545), ('xAswAru', 0.5), ('rAswAnu', 0.5), ('xAswAdu', 0.5) and the most similar Telugu words of the Kannada word *viBAgavu* are ('viBAgamu', 0.539), ('viBAga', 0.5), ('viBAgalanu', 0.467), ('viBAgamulu', 0.467).

We assume that for a Kannada word, its tags and their frequencies are equal to the most similar Telugu word. Based on this assumption, we build a lexicon for Kannada with each word having its plausible tags and frequencies derived from Telugu. This lexicon is used for estimating transition probabilities.

[6]We used Python n-gram package for approximate string matching: `http://packages.python.org/ngram/`

4.3.2 Source tags and target morphology

For each morphological set from the machine annotated Telugu corpora, we determine all its plausible fine-grained POS tags. For example, morphological set **n.n.sg..o** is associated with all the tags which satisfy the regular expression ***.n.n.sg..o**. Then for every word in Kannada, based on its morphology determined by the morphological analyser, we assign all the tags applicable, as learned from Telugu uniformly. The drawback of this approach is that the search space is large.

4.3.3 Target tags with uniform distribution

Instead of estimating emission probabilities from the cross language, we learn the plausible fine-grained tags of a given Kannada word from the machine annotated Kannada corpora (Step 1) and assume uniform distribution over all its tags. Though we learn the tags using the existing POS tagger, we do not use the information about tag frequencies, and hence we are not using the emission probabilities of the existing tagger. The existing tagger is just used to build a lexicon for Kannada.

Since we run the tagger on a large Kannada corpus, our lexicon contains most of the Kannada word forms and their corresponding POS and morphological information. This lexicon helps in removing the pipeline of (Avinesh and Karthik, 2007), thus building a high-speed tagger. Even, if some words are absent in the lexicon, TnT is well known to predict tags for unseen words based on the transition probabilities.

The advantage of this method over the previous is that the search space is drastically reduced.

4.3.4 Target emission probabilities

In this method, we learn the Kannada emission probabilities directly from the machine annotated Kannada corpora, i.e. we use the emission probabilities of the existing tagger. This helps us in estimating the upper-bound performance of the cross-lingual tagger when the transition probabilities are taken from Telugu.

Also, it helps in estimating the upper-bound performance of mono-lingual tagger when the transition probabilities are directly taken from Kannada. Our mono-lingual tagger will be robust, fast and as accurate as the existing mono-lingual tagger.

4.4 Step4: Final Tagger

We experimented with various TnT tagging models by selecting transition and emission probabilities from the Steps 2 and 3. Though one may question the performance of TnT for free-word order languages like Kannada, Hana et al. (2004) found that TnT models are as good as other models for free-word order languages. Additionally, Schmid and Laws (2008) observed that TnT models are also good at learning fined-grained transition probabilities. In our evaluation, we also found that our TnT models are competitive to the existing CRF model of (Avinesh and Karthik, 2007).

Apart from building POS tagging models, we also learned the associations of each word with its lemma and suffix given a POS tag, from the machine annotated Kannada corpus. For example, Kannada word *aramaneVgalYannu* is associated with lemma *aramaneV* and suffix *annu* when occurred with the tag NN.n.n.pl..o and similarly word *aramaneVgeV* is associated with lemma *aramaneV* and suffix *igeV* when occurred with the tag NN.n.n.sg..o.

An example sentence tagged by our models along with the lemmatisation is displayed in Figure 1.

5 Evaluation Results

We evaluated all our models on the manually annotated Kannada corpora developed by the ILMT consortium[7]. The corpus consists of 201,373 words and it is tagged with Bharati et al. (2006) tagset which forms the first field of our fine-grained POS tagset. Since we did not have manually annotated data for morphology, we evaluated only on the first field of our tags. For example, in the tag *NST.n.n.pl..o*, we evaluate only for *NST*.

Table 2 displays the results for various tagging models. Note that all our models are TnT models whereas (Avinesh and Karthik, 2007) is a CRF model.

Model 1 uses the transition probabilities of Telugu (section 4.2.1) and emission probabilities estimated from Telugu using approximate string matching (section 4.3.1). This model achieves 50% accuracy without using almost any resources of the target language. This is encouraging especially for languages which do not have any re-

[7]This corpus is not publicly available and is licensed. We did not use it for any of our training purposes except for the evaluation

Model	Transition Prob	Emission Prob	Precision	Recall	F-measure
		Cross-Language POS Tagger			
1	From the source language	Approximate string matching	56.88	56.88	56.88
2	From the source language	Source tags and target morphology	28.65	28.65	28.65
3	From the source language	Target tags with uniform distribution	75.10	75.10	75.10
4	From the source language	Target emission probabilities	77.63	77.63	77.63
		Mono-Lingual POS Tagger			
5	From the target language	Target emission probabilities	77.66	77.66	77.66
6	(Avinesh and Karthik, 2007)		78.64	61.48	69.01

Table 2: Evaluation results of various tagging models

sources.

Model 2 uses the transition probabilities of Telugu (section 4.2.1) and the emission probabilities estimated by mapping Telugu tags to the Kannada morphology (section 4.3.2). The performance is poor due to explosion in search space of the plausible tags. We optimise the search space using a Kannada lexicon in Model 3.

Model 3 uses the transition probabilities of Telugu (section 4.2.1) and emission probabilities estimated from machine-built Kannada lexicon (section 4.3.3). The performance is competitive with the mono-lingual taggers Models 5 and 6. The tagger has better F-measure than (Avinesh and Karthik, 2007). This model reveals that transition probabilities apply across typologically related Indian languages. To build an efficient cross-lingual tagger, it is good-enough to use cross-language transitions along with the target lexicon i.e. the list of all the tags plausible for a given target word.

Model 4 uses the transition probabilities of Telugu (section 4.2.1) and emission probabilities of Kannada estimated from the existing Kannada tagger (section 4.3.4). This gives us an idea of the upper-bound performance of cross-language POS taggers when source transition probabilities are used. The performance is almost equal to the mono-lingual tagger Model 5, showing that transition probabilities across Kannada and Telugu are almost same. We could build cross-language POS taggers as efficient as mono-lingual taggers conditioned that we have a good target lexicon.

Model 5 is a mono-lingual tagger which uses target transition and emission probabilities estimated from the existing tagger (section 4.2.2 and 4.3.4). The performance is highly competitive with better F-measure than (Avinesh and Karthik, 2007). This shows that a HMM-based tagger is as efficient as a CRF model (or any other model). While to tag 16 million words of Kannada corpora using (Avinesh and Karthik, 2007) took 5 days on a Quadcore processor @ 2.3 GHz each core, it hardly took few minutes by TnT model with better recall. We also aim to develop robust, fast and efficient mono-lingual taggers to Indian languages which already have POS taggers.

Table 3 displays the tagwise results of our cross-language tagger Model 3, our mono-lingual tagger Model 5 and the existing mono-lingual tagger Model 6.

6 Conclusions

This is an attempt to build POS taggers and other tools for resource-poor Indian languages using relatively resource-rich languages. Our experimental results for Kannada using Telugu are highly encouraging towards building cross-language tools. Cross-language POS taggers are found to be as accurate as the mono-lingual POS taggers.

Future directions include building cross language tools for other resource-poor Indian language, such as Malayalam using Tamil, Marathi using Hindi, Nepali using Hindi, etc. For Indian languages which already have tools, we aim to build robust, fast and efficient tools using the existing tools.

Finally, all the tools developed in this work are available for download[8]. The corpora (tagged) developed for this work is accessible through Sketch Engine[9] or Intellitext[10] interface.

Acknowledgements

This work has been supported by AHRC DEDEFI grant AH/H037306/1. Thanks to anonymous reviwers for thier useful feedback.

[8]The tools developed in this work can be downloaded from `http://sivareddy.in/downloads` or `http://corpus.leeds.ac.uk/serge/`

[9]Sketch Engine `http://sketchengine.co.uk`

[10]Intellitext `http://corpus.leeds.ac.uk/it/`

Tag	Freq	Prec	Recall	F1	Prec	Recall	F1	Prec	Recall	F1
		Model 3			Model 5			Model 6		
NN	81289	74.32	84.89	79.25	81.58	80.79	81.19	84.91	62.59	72.06
VM	33421	84.56	88.21	86.35	83.94	89.39	86.58	86.79	71.78	78.57
SYM	30835	92.26	95.51	93.86	95.57	96.11	95.84	95.64	73.99	83.43
JJ	13429	54.92	27.59	36.73	55.54	39.70	46.30	56.38	32.76	41.44
PRP	9102	60.02	33.14	42.70	59.07	56.01	57.50	60.69	46.07	52.38
QC	7699	90.70	73.45	81.17	90.55	93.52	92.01	88.52	70.40	78.43
NNP	7221	43.66	45.41	44.52	60.87	61.82	61.34	62.20	61.72	61.96
CC	4003	87.11	92.03	89.50	88.62	94.33	91.38	88.69	75.39	81.50
RB	3957	27.03	26.26	26.64	33.48	37.30	35.29	34.31	29.52	31.73
NST	2139	49.26	62.51	55.10	38.72	79.34	52.04	40.27	67.27	50.39
QF	1385	67.17	80.36	73.18	54.95	80.51	65.32	58.18	70.61	63.80
NEG	889	68.00	3.82	7.24	89.93	42.18	57.43	86.50	35.32	50.16
QO	622	54.66	20.74	30.07	45.43	28.78	35.24	54.00	21.70	30.96
WQ	599	70.25	46.91	56.26	80.17	80.30	80.23	81.73	55.26	65.94
PSP	374	7.92	2.14	3.37	-	-	-	26.28	71.39	38.42
INTF	23	5.32	43.48	9.48	5.08	60.00	9.38	1.06	17.39	2.00
INJ	3	5.13	66.67	9.52	1.67	33.33	3.17	2.70	33.33	5.00
Overall	201,373	75.10	75.10	75.10	77.66	77.66	77.66	78.64	61.48	69.01

Table 3: Tag wise results of Models 3, 5 and 6 described in Table 2

References

P.J. Antony and K.P. Soman. 2010. Kernel based part of speech tagger for kannada. In *Machine Learning and Cybernetics (ICMLC), 2010 International Conference on*, volume 4, pages 2139 –2144, july.

P.J. Antony, M Anand Kumar, and K.P. Soman. 2010. Paradigm based morphological analyzer for kannada language using machine learning approach. *Advances in Computational Sciences and Technology (ACST)*, 3(4).

Sue B. T. Atkins and Michael Rundell. 2008. *The Oxford Guide to Practical Lexicography*. Oxford University Press, Oxford.

P. V. S. Avinesh and G. Karthik. 2007. Part-Of-Speech Tagging and Chunking using Conditional Random Fields and Transformation-Based Learning. In *Proceedings of the IJCAI and the Workshop On Shallow Parsing for South Asian Languages (SPSAL)*, pages 21–24.

Akshar Bharati and Prashanth R. Mannem. 2007. Introduction to shallow parsing contest on south asian languages. In *Proceedings of the IJCAI and the Workshop On Shallow Parsing for South Asian Languages (SPSAL)*, pages pages 1–8.

A. Bharati, R. Sangal, D. M. Sharma, and L. Bai. 2006. Anncorra: Annotating corpora guidelines for pos and chunk annotation for indian languages. In *Technical Report (TR-LTRC-31), LTRC, IIIT-Hyderabad.*

A. Bharati, R. Sangal, and D.M. Sharma. 2007. Ssf: Shakti standard format guide. Technical Report TR-LTRC-33, Language Technologies Research Centre, IIIT-Hyderabad, India.

Thorsten Brants. 2000. Tnt: a statistical part-of-speech tagger. In *Proceedings of the sixth conference on Applied natural language processing*, ANLC '00, pages 224–231, Stroudsburg, PA, USA. Association for Computational Linguistics.

Andrei Z. Broder, Steven C. Glassman, Mark S. Manasse, and Geoffrey Zweig. 1997. Syntactic clustering of the web. In *Selected papers from the sixth international conference on World Wide Web*, pages 1157–1166.

Dipanjan Das and Slav Petrov. 2011. Unsupervised part-of-speech tagging with bilingual graph-based projections. In *Proceedings of ACL 2011.*

Amaresh Datta. 1998. *The Encyclopaedia Of Indian Literature*, volume 2.

Anna Feldman, Jirka Hana, and Chris Brew. 2006. A cross-language approach to rapid creation of new morpho-syntactically annotated resources. In *Proceedings of LREC*, pages 549–554.

Jiri Hana, Anna Feldman, and Chris Brew. 2004. A Resource-light Approach to Russian Morphology: Tagging Russian using Czech resources. In *Proceedings of EMNLP 2004*, Barcelona, Spain.

Adam Kilgarriff and Gregory Grefenstette. 2003. Introduction to the special issue on the web as corpus. *CL*, 29(3):333–348.

Adam Kilgarriff, Siva Reddy, Jan Pomikálek, and Avinesh PVS. 2010. A corpus factory for many languages. In *Proceedings of the Seventh conference on International Language Resources and Evaluation (LREC'10)*, Valletta, Malta, may. European Language Resources Association (ELRA).

Kavi Narayana Murthy. 2000. Computer processing of kannada language. Technical report, Computer and Kannada Development, Kannada University, Hampi.

Tahira Naseem, Benjamin Snyder, Jacob Eisenstein, and Regina Barzilay. 2009. Multilingual part-of-speech tagging: Two unsupervised approaches. *J. Artif. Intell. Res. (JAIR)*, 36:341–385.

Helmut Schmid and Florian Laws. 2008. Estimation of conditional probabilities with decision trees and an application to fine-grained pos tagging. In *Proceedings of the 22nd International Conference on Computational Linguistics - Volume 1*, COLING '08, pages 777–784, Stroudsburg, PA, USA. Association for Computational Linguistics.

B. R Shambhavi, P Ramakanth Kumar, K Srividya, B J Jyothi, Spoorti Kundargi, and G Varsha Shastri. 2011. Kannada morphological analyser and generator using trie. *IJCSNS International Journal of Computer Science and Network Security*, 11(1), January.

Benjamin Snyder, Tahira Naseem, Jacob Eisenstein, and Regina Barzilay. 2008. Unsupervised multilingual learning for pos tagging. In *Proceedings of the Conference on Empirical Methods in Natural Language Processing*, EMNLP '08, pages 1041–1050, Stroudsburg, PA, USA. Association for Computational Linguistics.

T. N. Vikram and Shalini R. Urs. 2007. Development of prototype morphological analyzer for the south indian language of kannada. In *Proceedings of the 10th international conference on Asian digital libraries: looking back 10 years and forging new frontiers*, ICADL'07, pages 109–116, Berlin, Heidelberg. Springer-Verlag.

David Yarowsky and Grace Ngai. 2001. Inducing multilingual pos taggers and np bracketers via robust projection across aligned corpora. In *Proceedings of the second meeting of the North American Chapter of the Association for Computational Linguistics on Language technologies*, NAACL '01, pages 1–8, Stroudsburg, PA, USA. Association for Computational Linguistics.

David Yarowsky, Grace Ngai, and Richard Wicentowski. 2001. Inducing multilingual text analysis tools via robust projection across aligned corpora. In *Proceedings of the first international conference on Human language technology research*, HLT '01, pages 1–8, Stroudsburg, PA, USA. Association for Computational Linguistics.

Integrate Multilingual Web Search Results using Cross-Lingual Topic Models

Duo Ding
Shanghai Jiao Tong University, Shanghai, 200240, P.R. China
dingduo1@gmail.com

Abstract

With the thriving of the Internet, web users today have access to resources around the world in more than 200 different languages. How to effectively manage multilingual web search results has emerged as an essential problem. In this paper, we introduce the ongoing work of leveraging a Cross-Lingual Topic Model (CLTM) to integrate the multilingual search results. The CLTM detects the underlying topics of different language results and uses the topic distribution of each result to cluster them into topic-based classes. In CLTM, we unify distributions in topic level by direct translation, thus distinguishing from other multilingual topic models, which mainly concern the parallelism at document or sentence level (Mimno 2009; Ni, 2009). Experimental results suggest that our CLTM clustering method is effective and outperforms the 6 compared clustering approaches.

1 Introduction

The growing of the Internet has made the web multilingual. With the Internet, user can browse the web page written in any language, and search for results in any language in the world.

However, since users would have a large set of search results edited in many languages after multilingual search (shown as Figure 1), the redundancy issue became a problem. Here the "redundancy issue" stands for two problems. The first is that we would get duplicated results from different language search. This can be fixed by simply maintaining a set and throw away the duplicated results. The second problem is that the users will get so many search results after multilingual search that they cannot quickly find the results they want. To facilitate users' quick browsing, one effective solution might be post-retrieval document clustering, which had been shown by Hearst and Pedersen (1996) to produce superior results. So we can employ the Cross-Lingual Topic Models to cluster the numerous results into topic classes, each containing the results related to one specific topic, to solve the redundancy problem.

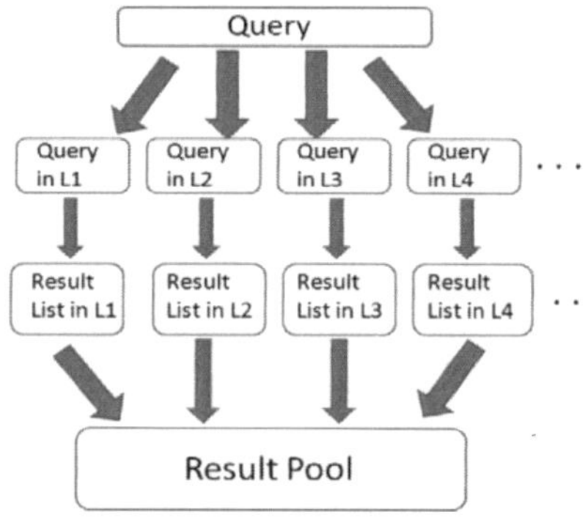

Figure 1: Multilingual Search

Our approach works in two steps. First we translate the topic documents into a unified language. Then, by conducting a clustering method derived from the Cross-Lingual Topic Model (CLTM), we cluster all the results into topic classes. We assume different "topics" exist among all the returned search results. (Blei 2003). Thus by detecting the underlying topics of search results, we give a topic distribution for each result and then cluster it into a particular class according to the distribution. Through experiments, the CLTM gives an impressive performance in clustering multilingual web search results.

2 Cross-Lingual Topic Models

Topic models have emerged as a very useful tool to detect underlying topics of text collections. They are probabilistic models for uncovering the underlying semantic structure of a document collection

Proceedings of the 5th International Joint Conference on Natural Language Processing, pages 20–24, Chiang Mai, Thailand, November 8-12, 2011.

based on a hierarchical Bayesian analysis of the original texts (Blei et al. 2003). Having the method of assigning topic distributions to the terms and documents, this analysis of the context can be utilized on many applications. Meanwhile, the development of multilingual search is calling for useful cross-lingual tools to integrate the results in different languages. So we leverage Cross-Lingual Topic Models (CLTM) to accomplish the task of integrating multilingual web results.

Some similar methods have been proposed recently to define polylingual or multilingual topic models to find the topics aligned across multiple languages (Mimno 2009; Ni, 2009). The key difference between us is that the polylingual topic models assume that the documents in a tuple share the individual tuple-specific distribution over topics, while in the Cross-Lingual Topic Model, the distributions of tuples and different languages are identical. At the same time, our emphasis is to utilize the power of CLTM to solve the problem of clustering multilingual search results, which is different from other topic model tools.

2.1 Definition

Firstly we give the statistical assumptions and terminology in Cross-Lingual Topic Models (CLTM). The thought behind CLTM is that, for results within a specific language search result set, we model each result as arising from multiple topics, where a topic is defined to be a distribution over a fixed vocabulary of terms in this language. In every language Li, Let K be a specified number of topics, V the size of the vocabulary, $\vec{\alpha}$ a positive K-vector, and η a scalar. We let DirV ($\vec{\alpha}$) denote a V-dimensional Dirichlet with vector parameter $\vec{\alpha}$ and DirK (η) denote a K dimensional symmetric Dirichlet with scalar parameter η.

There might be several topics underlying in the collection. We draw a distribution for each topic over words $\vec{\beta}_k \sim \mathrm{Dir}_V(\eta)$. And for each search result document, we draw a vector of topic proportions $\vec{\theta}_d \sim \mathrm{Dir}(\vec{\alpha})$. Finally for each word, we firstly give a topic assignment $Z_{d,n} \sim \mathrm{Mult}(\vec{\theta}_d)$, where the range of $Z_{d,n}$ is 1 to K; then draw a word $W_{d,n} \sim \mathrm{Mult}(\vec{\beta}_{z_{d,n}})$, where the range of $W_{d,n}$ is from 1 to V.

From definition above we can see that the hidden topical structure of a collection is represented in the hidden random variables: the topics $\vec{\beta}_{1:K}$, the per-document topic proportions $\vec{\theta}_{1:D}$, and the per-word topic assignments $z_{1:D,1:N}$. This is similar to another kind of topic models, latent Dirichlet allocation (LDA).

We make central use of the Dirichlet distribution in CLTM, the exponential family distribution over the simplex of positive vectors that sum to one. Since we use distribution similar to latent Dirichlet allocation on each language result set, we give the Dirichlet density:

$$p(\theta \mid \vec{\alpha}) = \frac{\Gamma\left(\sum_i \alpha_i\right)}{\prod_i \Gamma(\alpha_i)} \prod_i \theta_i^{\alpha_i - 1} \qquad (1)$$

The parameter $\vec{\alpha}$ is a positive K-vector, and Γ denotes the Gamma function, which can be thought of as a real-valued extension of the factorial function. Under the assumption that document collections (result sets) in different languages share a same topic distribution, we can describe the Cross-Lingual Topic Models in Figure 2.

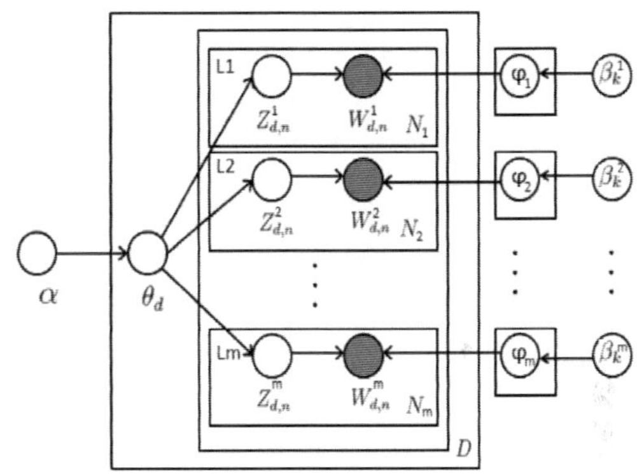

Figure 2: The graphical model presentation of the Cross-Lingual Topic Model (CLTM)

2.2 Clustering with CLTM

From the definition, we see that CLTM contains two Dirichlet random variables: the topic proportions $\vec{\theta}$ are distributions over topic indices {1, . . . , K}; the topics $\widehat{\beta}$ are distributions over the vocabulary. We use these variables to formulate our topic-detecting method.

Detecting Topics

In CLTM, exploring a corpus through a topic model typically begins with visualizing the posterior topics through their per-topic term probabilities $\widehat{\beta}$. In our method, we need to find several topics in the "Result Pool" of each query, thus making it possible to assign topic distributions to each result in the set. To do so, we detect the topics in a result set by visualizing several posterior topics and use the following formula to calculate the word score:

$$\text{word-score}_{k,v} = \widehat{\beta}_{k,v} \log \left(\frac{\widehat{\beta}_{k,v}}{\left(\prod_{j=1}^{K} \widehat{\beta}_{j,v} \right)^{\frac{1}{K}}} \right) \quad (2)$$

We can see that the above formula is based on the TFIDF term score of vocabulary terms used in information retrieval (Baeza-Yates and Rbiero-Neto, 1999). We use this score to determine salient topics in a query's result set. The first part of it is similar to the term frequency (TF); the second part is similar to the document frequency (IDF).

Document Topic Distribution

When several topics are found in a result set, we would like to know the underlying topics contained in each result document so that we can cluster them into a particular class according to their topics. Since a result document may contain multiple topics and what we need is the most salient one, we can plot the posterior topic proportions and examine the most likely topic assigned to each word in this query to find the most salient topic. In our method, we sum up the distribution of every term in the document to form the final distribution of this doc.

$$\text{doc-score}_{k,v} = \sum_{i=1}^{N_v} \widehat{\beta}_{i,v} \quad (3)$$

This formula calculates the similarity of a document on the *K*th topic. N*v* denotes quantity of words that the *v*th result contains.

After the two-step processing, for each result document in a query's result list, we have *K* similarities which respectively denote the possibility for the document to be clustered to the *K*th topic class. We then conduct clustering on the result set based on this possibility to put them in different topic-based classes.

3 Experiments

In this section, we give experimental results on Cross-Lingual Topic Model clustering method, compared with 6 other clustering algorithms, to show that CLTM is a powerful tool in cross-lingual context analysis and multilingual topic-based clustering.

For this series of experiments we simply use the cluster results of two languages, English and Chinese to show the performance of different clustering methods (Because it is convenient to evaluate). However, due to the fact that the Cross-Lingual Topic Models are language independent, we believe that the method is also feasible in other languages.

3.1 Baseline Clustering Algorithms

In the first place, we apply 6 baseline clustering algorithms to the unified search results. We extract 20 frequently referred Chinese search queries and translate them into English. (Using Google Translate.) Then for each pair of queries we search them both in Chinese and English in the Google Search Engine, each recording top 40 returned results (including title, snippet and url). And then we regard English as the unified language and translate the 40 Chinese results into English, again using Google Translate, thus having totally 80 returned search results for each query.

In the next step, for each of the 80 results, we convert these 80 snippets into the vector-space format files. After that, we begin to cluster these result documents (snippets) into classes. In our definition, the cluster number is 5. The fixed-predefined clustering number is more effective for both baseline methods and CLTM method to conduct clustering and also drives it clearer to make comparisons.

The 6 baseline clustering algorithms we use are: repeated bisection (rb), refined repeated bisection (rbr), direct clustering (direct), agglomerative clustering (agglo), graph partitioning (graph), biased agglomerative (bagglo). We use a clustering tool, CLUTO, to implement baseline clustering.

The similarity function is chosen to be cosine function, and the clustering criterion function for the rb, rbr, and direct methods is

$$\text{maximize} \sum_{i=1}^{k} \sqrt{\sum_{v,u \in S_i} \text{sim}(v,u)} \quad (4)$$

In this formula, *K* is the total number of clusters, *S* is the total objects to be clustered, *Si* is the set of objects assigned to the *i*th cluster, *ni* is the number of objects in the *i*th cluster, *v* and *u* represent two objects, and *sim(v, u)* is the similarity between two objects.

Clustering Algorithm	Parameter	Algorithm Description
Repeated Bisection	-rb	The desired k-way clustering solution is computed by performing a sequence of k-1 repeated bisections.
Refined Repeated Bisection	-rbr	Similar to the above method, but at the end, the overall solution is globally optimized.
Direct Clustering	-direct	In this method, the desired k-way clustering solution is computed by simultaneously finding all k clusters.
Agglomerative Clustering	-agglo	The k-way clustering solution is computed using the agglomerative paradigm whose goal is to locally optimize (min or max) a particular clustering criterion function.
Graph Partitioning	-grapg	The clustering solution is computed by first modeling the objects using a nearest-neighbor graph, and then splitting the graph into k-clusters using a min-cut graph partitioning algorithm
Biased Agglomerative	-bagglo	Similar to the agglo method, but the agglomeration process is biased by a partitional clustering solution that is initially computed on the dataset.

Table 1: Parameter and description of the 6 baseline clustering algorithms used in the experiment

For agglomerative and biased agglomerative clustering algorithm, we use the traditional UPGMA criterion function and for graph partitioning algorithm, we use cluster-weighted single-link criterion function. The parameters and explanations for each clustering algorithm are represented in Table 1.

3.2 Cross-Lingual Topic Model Clustering

In Cross-Lingual Topic Model based clustering, we firstly calculate the word score for each vocabulary by using formula (2) in Section 2. Thus for each query, there is a probability for each of its vocabulary word on 5 different topics. Then, we use formula (3) to calculate the probability of each document (each snippet) on 5 topics. Finally, we find the topic with highest probability in each document and assign the document into this topic class, which finishes the process of clustering.

In our evaluation process, we ask 7 evaluators to view the results of different clustering methods. Each of the evaluators is given the clustering results on 2 or 3 queries in 7 different methods (6 baseline methods plus CLTM). And they are asked to compare the results by giving two scores to each method. In the evaluation process, they are blind to the clustering method names of the assigned results. The first score is the "Internal Similarity", which accounts for the similarity of the results clustered into the same class. This score reveals the compactness of each topic class and the range of the score is from 1 to 10: 1 score means not good compactness and 10 scores means perfect compactness. The second score is called "External Distinctness", which shows whether the classes are distinct with each other. The range is also 1 to 10: 1 score represents poor quality and 10 represents the best performance. The results of evaluations are shown in Figure 3 and Figure 4.

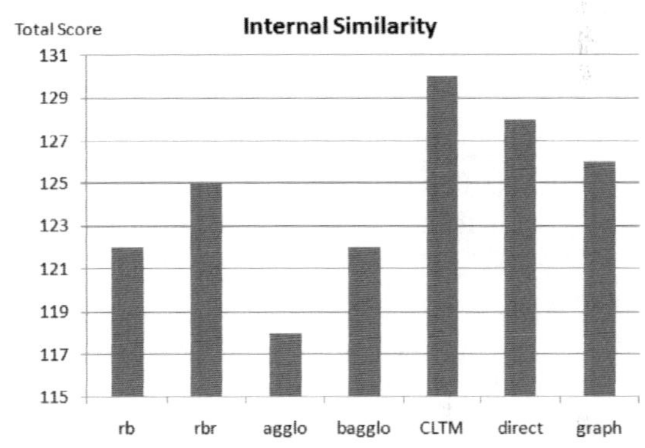

Figure 3: The Internal Similarity of 7 methods

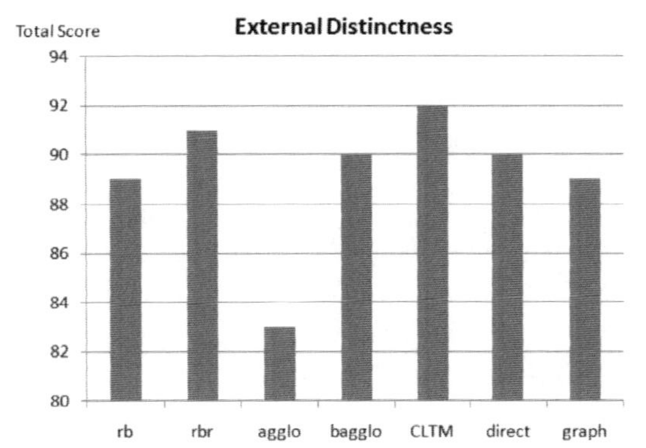

Figure 4: The External Distinctness of 7 methods

4 Conclusion

In this paper, we introduce the ongoing work of exploiting a kind of topic models, Cross-Lingual

Topic Models (CLTM), to solve the problem of integrating and clustering multilingual search results. The CLTM detects the underlying topics of the results and assign a distribution to each result. According to this distribution, we cluster each result to the topic class of which it is mainly about. We give each word a "word-score" which represents the distribution of topics on this word and sum all the term probabilities up in a result to obtain the topic distribution for each result document. To evaluate the effectiveness of Cross-Lingual Topic Models, we compare it with 6 baseline clustering algorithms on the same dataset. The experimental results of "Internal Similarity" and "External Distinctness" scores suggest that the Cross-Lingual Topic Model gives a better performance and provides more reasonable results for clustering multilingual web search documents.

Acknowledgments

The author would like to thank Matthew Scott of Microsoft Research Asia for helpful suggestions and comments. The author also thanks the anonymous reviewers for their insightful feedback.

References

Andreas Faatz: Enrichment Evaluation, technical report TR-AF-01-02 at Darmstadt University of Technology

A. V. Leouski and W. B. Croft. 1996. An evaluation of techniques for clustering search results. Technical Report IR-76, Department of Computer Science, University of Massachusetts, Amherst.

Bernard J. Jansen, Amanda Spink,*, Tefko Saracevic. 2000. Real life, real users, and real needs: a study and analysis of user queries on the web. Information Processing and Management 36 (2000).

Chi Lang Ngo and Hung Son Nguyen. 2004. A Tolerance Rough Set Approach to Clustering Web Search Results, PKDD 2004, LNAI 3202, pp. 515–517.

David Blei, Andrew Ng, and Michael Jordan. 2003. Latent Dirichlet allocation, 3:993-1022.

D. R. Cutting, D. R. Karger, J. O. Pedersen and J. W. Tukey, Scatter/Gather. 1992. A cluster-based approach to browsing large document collections, In *Proceedings of the 15th International ACM SIGIR Conference (SIGIR'92),* pp 318-329.

David Mimno, Hanna M. Wallach, Jason Naradowsky, David A. Smith and Andrew McCallum. 2009. Polylingual Topic Models, In *Proceedings of the 2009 Conference on Empirical Methods in Natural Language Processing*, pages 880–889, Singapore.

He Xiaoning, Wang Peidong, Qi Haoliang, Yang Muyun, Lei Guohua, Xue Yong. 2008. Using Google Translation in Cross-Lingual Information Retrieval, *Proceedings of NTCIR-7 Workshop Meeting,* December 16–19, Tokyo, Japan

Hua-Jun Zeng, Qi-Cai He, Zheng Chen, Wei-Ying Ma and Jinwen Ma. 2004. Learning to Cluster Web Search Results. SIGIR04, Sheffield, South Yorkshire, UK.

Liddle, S., Embley, D., Scott, D., Yau, S. 2002. Extracting Data Behind Web. In *Proceedings of the Joint Workshop on Conceptual Modeling Approaches for E-business: A Web Service Perspective (eCOMO 2002)*, pp. 38–49 (October 2002)

Murata, M, Ma, Q, and Isahara, H. 2002. "Applying multiple characteristics and techniques to obtain high levels of performance in information retrieval". *Proceedings of the Third NTCIR Workshop on Research in Information Retrieval, Question Answering and Summarization*, Tokyo Japan. NII, Tokyo.

McRoy, S. 1992. Using Multiple Knowledge Sources for Word Sense Discrimination, in Computational Linguistics, vol. 18, no. 1.

Peter F. Brown, Stephen A. Della Pietra, Vincent J. Della Pietra, Robert L. Mercer. 1993. The Mathematics of Statistical Machine Translation: Parameter Estimation. Computational Linguistics, volume 19, Issue 2.

P.S. Bradley, Usama Fayyad, and Cory Reina. 1998. Scaling Clustering Algorithms to Large Databases, From: KDD-98 Proceedings, AAAI (www.aaai.org).

Raghavan, S., Garcia-Molina, H. 2001. Crawling the Hidden Web. In: *Proceedings of the 27th International Conference on Very Large Data Bases*, pp.29–138.

W. B. Croft. 1978. Organizing and searching large files of documents, Ph.D. Thesis, University of Cambridge.

Xiaochuan Ni, Jian-Tao Sun, Jian Hu, and Zheng Chen. 2009. Mining Multilingual Topics from Wikipedia, WWW 2009, Madrid, Spain.

Zamir O., Etzioni O. 1998. Web Document Clustering: A Feasibility Demonstration, *Proceedings of the 19th International ACM SIGIR Conference on Research and Development of Information Retrieval (SIGIR'98)*, 46-54.

Zamir O., Etzioni O. Grouper. 1999. A Dynamic Clustering Interface to Web Search Results. In *Proceedings of the Eighth International World Wide Web Conference (WWW8)*, Toronto, Canada.

Soundex-based Translation Correction in Urdu–English Cross-Language Information Retrieval

Manaal Faruqui
Computer Science & Engg.
Indian Institute of Technology
Kharagpur, India
manaalfar@gmail.com

Prasenjit Majumder
Computer Science & Engg.
DAIICT Gandhinagar
Gandhinagar, India
p_majumder@daiict.ac.in

Sebastian Padó
Computational Linguistics
Heidelberg University
Heidelberg, Germany
pado@cl.uni-heidelberg.de

Abstract

Cross-language information retrieval is difficult for languages with few processing tools or resources such as Urdu. An easy way of translating content words is provided by Google Translate, but due to lexicon limitations named entities (NEs) are transliterated letter by letter. The resulting NEs errors (*zynydyny zdn* for *Zinedine Zidane*) hurts retrieval. We propose to replace English non-words in the translation output. First, we determine phonetically similar English words with the Soundex algorithm. Then, we choose among them by a modified Levenshtein distance that models correct transliteration patterns. This strategy yields an improvement of 4% MAP (from 41.2 to 45.1, monolingual 51.4) on the FIRE-2010 dataset.

1 Introduction

Cross-language information retrieval (CLIR) research is the study of systems that accept queries in one language and return text documents in a different language. CLIR is of considerable practical importance in countries with many languages like India. One of the most widely used languages is Urdu, the official language of five Indian states as well as the national language of Pakistan. There are around 60 million speakers of Urdu – 48 million in India and 11 million in Pakistan (Lewis, 2009).

Despite this large number of speakers, NLP for Urdu is still at a fairly early stage (Hussain, 2008). Studies have been conducted on POS tagging (Sajjad and Schmid, 2009), corpus construction (Becker and Riaz, 2002), word segmentation (Durrani and Hussain, 2010), lexicographic sorting (Hussain et al., 2007), and information extraction (Mukund et al., 2010). Many other processing tasks are still missing, and the size of the Urdu internet is minuscule compared to English and other major languages, making Urdu a prime candidate for a CLIR source language.

A particular challenge which Urdu poses for CLIR is its writing system. Even though it is a Central Indo-Aryan language and closely related to Hindi, its development was shaped predominantly by Persian and Arabic, and it is written in Perso-Arabic script rather than Devanagari. CLIR with a target language that uses another script needs to transliterate (Knight and Graehl, 1998) any material that cannot be translated (typically out-of-vocabulary items like Named Entities). The difficulties of Perso-Arabic in this respect are (a), some vowels are represented by letters which are also consonants and (b), short vowels are customarily omitted. For example, in ونونا (*Winona*) the first و is used for the *W* but the second is used for *O*. Also the *i* sound is missing after و (*W*).

In this paper, we consider Urdu–English CLIR. Starting from a readily available baseline (using Google Translate to obtain English queries), we show that transliteration of Named Entities, more specifically missing vowels, is indeed a major factor in wrongly answered queries. We reconstruct missing vowels in an unsupervised manner through an approximate string matching procedure based on phonetic similarity and orthographic similarity by using Soundex code (Knuth, 1975) and Levenshtein distance (Gusfield, 1997) respectively, and find a clear improvement over the baseline.

2 Translation Strategies for Urdu–English

We present a series of strategies for translating Urdu queries into English so that they can be pre-

Proceedings of the 5th International Joint Conference on Natural Language Processing, pages 25–29,
Chiang Mai, Thailand, November 8-12, 2011.

sented to a monolingual English IR system that works on some English document collection. Inspection of the strategies' errors led us to develop a hierarchy of increasingly sophisticated strategies.

2.1 Baseline model (GTR)

As our baseline, we aimed for a model that is state-of-the-art, freely available, and can be used by users without the need for heavy computational machinery. We decided to render the Urdu query into English with the Google Translate web service.[1]

2.2 Approximate Matching (GTR+SoEx)

Google Translate appears to have a limited Urdu lexicon. Words that are out of vocabulary (OOV) are transliterated letter by letter into the Latin alphabet. Without an attempt to restore short (unwritten) vowels, these match the actual English terms only very rarely. For example, *Singur*, the name of a village in India gets translated to *Sngur*.

To address this problem, we attempt to map these incomplete transliterations onto well-formed English words using approximate string matching. We use Soundex (Knuth, 1975), an algorithm which is normally used for "phonetic normalization". Soundex maps English words onto their first letter plus three digits which represent equivalence classes over consonants, throwing away all vowels in the process. For example, *Ashcraft* is mapped onto A261, where 2 stands for the "gutturals" and "sibilants" S and K, 6 for R, and 1 for the "labiodental" F. All codes beyond the first three are ignored. The same soundex code would be assigned, for example, to *Ashcroft*, *Ashcrop*, or even *Azaroff*. The two components which make Soundex a well-suited choice for our purposes are exactly (a), the forming of equivalence classes over consonants, which counteracts variance introduced by one-to-many correspondences between Latin and Arabic letters; and (b), the omission of vowels.

Specifically, we use Soundex as a hash function, mapping all English words from our English document collection onto their Soundex codes. The GTR+SoEx model then attempts to correct all words in the Google Translate output by replacing them with the English word sharing the same Soundex code that has the highest frequency in the English document collection.

[1] http://translate.google.com. All queries were translated in the first week of January 2011.

2.3 NER-centered Approximate Matching (GTR+SoExNER)

An analysis of the output of the GTR+SoEx model showed that the model indeed ensured that all words in the translation were English words, but that it "overcorrected", replacing correctly translated, but infrequent, English words by more frequent words with the same Soundex code. Unfortunately, Google Translate does not indicate which words in its output are out-of-vocabulary.

Recall that our original motivation was to improve coverage specifically for out-of-vocabulary words, virtually all of which are Named Entities. Thus, we decided to apply Soundex matching only to NEs. As a practical and simple way of identifying malformed NEs, we considered those words in the Google Translate output which did not occur in the English document base at all (i.e., which were "non-words"). We manually verified that this heuristic indeed identified malformed Named Entities in our experimental materials (see Section 3 below for details). We found a recall of 100% (all true NEs were identified) and a precision of 96% (a small number of non-NEs was classified as NEs).

The GTR+SoExNER strategy applies Soundex matching to all NEs, but not to other words in the Google Translate output.

2.4 Disambiguation (GTR+SoExNER+LD(mod))

Generally, a word that has been wrongly transliterated from Urdu maps onto the same Soundex code as several English words. The median number of English words per transliteration is 7. This can be seen as a sort of ambiguity, and the strategy adopted by the previous models is to just choose the most frequent candidate, similar to the "predominant" sense baseline in word sense disambiguation (McCarthy et al., 2004). We found however that the most frequent candidate is often wrong, since Soundex conflates fairly different words (cf. Section 2.2). For example, *Subhas*, the first name of an Indian freedom fighter, receives the soundex code *S120* but it is mapped onto the English term *Space* ($freq$=7243) instead of *Subhas* ($freq$=2853).

We therefore experimented with a more informed strategy that chooses the English candidate based on two variants of Levenshtein distance. The first model, GTR+SoExNER+LD, uses standard Levenshtein distance with a cost of 1 for each insertion, deletion and substitution. Our final model, `GTR+SoExNER+LDmod` uses a modified version of Levenshtein distance which is optimized to model the correspondences that we expect. Specifically, the addition of vowels and the replacement of consonants by vowels come with no cost, to favour the recovery of English vowels that are unexpressed in Urdu or expressed as consonants (cf. Section 1). Thus, the `LDmod` between *zdn* and *zidane* would be Zero.

3 Experimental Setup

Document Collection and Queries Our experiments are based on the FIRE-2010[2] English data, consisting of documents and queries, as our experimental materials. The document collection consists of about 124,000 documents from the English-language newspaper "The Telegraph India"[3] from 2004-07. The average length of a document was 40 words. The FIRE query collection consists of 50 English queries which were of the same domain as that of the document collection. The average number of relevant documents for a query was 76 (with a minimum of 13 and a maximum of 228).

The first author, who has an advanced knowledge of Urdu, translated the English FIRE queries manually into Urdu. One of the resulting Urdu query is shown in Table 1, together with the Google translations back into English (GTR) which form the basis of the CLIR queries in the simplest model. Every query has a *title*, and a *description*, both of which we used for retrieval. The bottom row (*entity*) shows the Translate output and from the best model (Soundex matching with modified Levenshtein distance). The bold-faced terms correspond to names that are corrected successfully, increasing the query's precision from 49% to 86%.

Cross-lingual IR setup We implemented the models described in Section 2, using the Terrier IR engine (Ounis et al., 2006) for retrieval from the FIRE-2010 English document collection. We used the PL2 weighting model with the term frequecy normalisation parameter of 10.99. The document collection and the queries were stemmed using the Porter Stemmer (Porter, 1980). We applied all translation strategies defined in Section 2 as *query expansion* modules that enrich the Google Translate output with new relevant query terms. In a pre-experiment, we experimented with adding either only the single most similar term for each OOV item (1-best) or the best n terms (n-best). We consistently found better results for 1-best and report results for this condition only.

Monolingual model We also computed a monolingual English model which did not use the translated Urdu queries but the original English ones instead. The result for this model can be seen as an upper bound for Urdu-English CLIR models.

Evaluation We report two evaluation measures. The first one is Mean Average Precision (MAP), an evaluation measure that is highest when all correct items are ranked at the top (Manning et al., 2008). MAP measures the global quality of the ranked document list; however improvements in MAP could result from an improved treatment of marginally relevant documents, while it is the quality of the top-ranked documents that is most important in practice and correlates best with extrinsic measures (Scholer and Turpin, 2009). Therefore we also consider P@5, the precision of the five top-ranked documents.

4 Results and Discussion

Table 2 shows the results of our experiments. Monolingual English retrieval achieves a MAP of 51.4, while the CLIR baseline (Google Translate only – GTR) is 41.3. We expect the results of our experiments to fall between these two extremes.

We first extend the baseline model with Soundex matching for all terms in the title and description (`GTR+SoEx`), we actually obtain a result way below the baseline (MAP=36.7). The reason is that, as discussed in Section 2.2, Soundex is too coarse-grained for non-NEs, grouping words such as *red* and *road* into the same equivalence class, thus pulling in irrelevant terms. This analysis is supported by the observation, mentioned above, that 1-best always performs better than n-best.

We are however able to obtain a clear improvement of about 1.5% absolute by limiting Soundex matching to automatically identified Named Entities, up to MAP=43.0 (`GTR+SoExNER`). However, this model still relies completely on frequency for choosing among competitors with the same Soundex code, leading to errors like the *Subhas/Space* mixup discusssed in Section 2.4. The use of Levenshtein distance, representing a more informed manner of disambiguation, makes

[2]`http://www.isical.ac.in/~fire/2010/data_download.html`

[3]`http://www.telegraphindia.com/`

title UR title EN (GTR)	زینیدین زیدان کا ورلڈ کپ میں سر سے مارنے کا واقعہ Zynydyny zydan World Cup head butt incident
desc UR desc EN (GTR)	ایسے دستاویزات کو تلاش کریں جس میں زیدان نے ماتیرزّی کو سر سے ورلڈ کپ ۲۰۰۶ کے فاءینل میں مارا جب اتالوی نے زیدان کے خلاف ناگوار باتیں بولیں Find these documents from public opinion zdn to mtrzzy, from Italian to zydan about offensive comments, World Cup finals in 2006 head to kill incidents are mentioned
entity EN (GTR) entity (GTR+SoExNER+LDmod)	Zynydyny Zydan zdn Mtrzzy **zinedine** zaydan **zidane materazzi**

Table 1: A sample query

Model	MAP	P@5
GTR	41.3	62.4
GTR+SoEx	36.7	59.2
GTR+SoExNER	43.0	62.4
GTR+SoExNER+LD	45.0	65.2
GTR+SoExNER+LDmod	**45.3**	**65.6**
Monolingual English	51.4	71.6

Table 2: Results for Urdu-English CLIR models on the FIRE 2010 collection (Mean Average Precision and Precision of top five documents)

a considerable difference, and leads to a final MAP of 45.33 or about 4% absolute increase for the (`GTR+SoExNER+LDmod`) model. A bootstrap resampling analysis (Efron and Tibshirani, 1994) confirmed that the difference between `GTR+SoExNER+LDmod` and `GTR` model is significant ($p<0.05$). All models are still significantly worse than the monolingual English model.

The P@5 results are in tandem with the MAP results for all models, showing that the improvement which we obtain for the best model leads to top-5 lists whose precision is on average more than 3% better than the baseline top-5 lists. This difference is not significant, but we attribute the absence of significance to the small sample size (50 queries).

In a qualitative analysis, we found that many remaining low-MAP queries still suffer from missing or incorrect Named Entities. For example, *Noida* (an industrial area near New Delhi), was transliterated to *Nuydh* and then incorrectly modified to *Nidhi* (an Indian name). This case demonstrates the limits of our method which cannot distinguish well among NEs which differ mainly in their vowels.

5 Related Work

There are several areas of related work. The first is IR in Urdu, where monolingual work has been done (Riaz, 2008). However, to our knowledge, our study is the first one to address Urdu CLIR. The second is machine transliteration, which is a widely researched area (Knight and Graehl, 1998) but which usually requires some sort of bilingual resource. Knight and Graehl (1998) use 8000 English-Japanese place name pairs, and Mandal et al. (2007) hand-code rules for Hindi and Bengali to English. In contrast, our method does not require any bilingual resources. Finally, Soundex codes have been applied to Thai-English CLIR (Suwanvisat and Prasitjutrakul, 1998) and Arabic name search (Aqeel et al., 2006). They have also been found useful for indexing Named Entities (Raghavan and Allan, 2004; Kondrak, 2004) as well as IR more generally (Holmes and McCabe, 2002).

6 Conclusion

In this paper, we have considered CLIR from Urdu into English. With Google Translate as translation system, the biggest hurdle is that most named entities are out-of-vocabulary items and transliterated incorrectly. A simple, completely unsupervised postprocessing strategy that replaces English nonwords by phonetically similar words with minimal edit distance is able to recover almost half of the loss in MAP that the cross-lingal setup incurs over a monolingual English one. Directions for future work include monolingual query expansion in Urdu to improve the non-NE part of the query and training a full Urdu-English transliteration system.

Acknowledgments We thank A. Tripathi and H. Sajjad for invaluable discussions and suggestions.

References

Syed Uzair Aqeel, Steve Beitzel, Eric Jensen, David Grossman, and Ophir Frieder. 2006. On the development of name search techniques for Arabic. *Journal of the American Society for Information Science and Technology*, 57(6):728–739.

Dara Becker and Kashif Riaz. 2002. A study in urdu corpus construction. In *Proceedings of the 3rd COLING workshop on Asian language resources and international standardization*, pages 1–5, Taipei, Taiwan.

Nadir Durrani and Sarmad Hussain. 2010. Urdu word segmentation. In *Proceedings of the Annual Conference of the North American Chapter of the Association for Computational Linguistics*, pages 528–536, Los Angeles, California.

Bradley Efron and Robert Tibshirani. 1994. *An Introduction to the Bootstrap*. Monographs on Statistics and Applied Probability 57. Chapman & Hall.

Dan Gusfield. 1997. *Algorithms on strings, trees, and sequences: computer science and computational biology*. Cambridge University Press, Cambridge, UK.

David Holmes and M. Catherine McCabe. 2002. Improving precision and recall for soundex retrieval. In *Proceedings of the International Conference on Information Technology: Coding and Computing*, pages 22–27, Washington, DC, USA.

Sarmad Hussain, Sana Gul, and Afifah Waseem. 2007. Developing lexicographic sorting: An example for urdu. *ACM Transactions on Asian Language Information Processing*, 6(3):10:1–10:17.

Sarmad Hussain. 2008. Resources for urdu language processing. In *Proceedings of the Workshop on Asian Language Resources at IJCNLP 2008*, Hyderabad, India.

Kevin Knight and Jonathan Graehl. 1998. Machine transliteration. *Computational Linguistics*, 24(4):599–612.

Donald E. Knuth. 1975. *Fundamental Algorithms*, volume III of *The Art of Computer Programming*. Addison-Wesley, Reading, MA.

Grzegorz Kondrak. 2004. Identification of confusable drug names: A new approach and evaluation methodology. In *In Proceedings of the International Conference on Computational Linguistics*, pages 952–958, Geneva, Switzerland.

M. Paul Lewis, editor. 2009. *Ethnologue – Languages of the World*. SIL International, 16th edition.

Debasis Mandal, Mayank Gupta, Sandipan Dandapat, Pratyush Banerjee, and Sudeshna Sarkar. 2007. Bengali and Hindi to English CLIR evaluation. In *Proceedings of CLEF*, pages 95–102.

Christopher D. Manning, Prabhakar Raghavan, and Hinrich Schütze. 2008. *Introduction to Information Retrieval*. Cambridge University Press, Cambridge, UK, 1st edition.

Diana McCarthy, Rob Koeling, Julie Weeds, and John Carroll. 2004. Finding predominant senses in untagged text. In *Proceedings of the Annual Meeting of the Association for Computational Linguistics*, pages 280–287, Barcelona, Spain.

Smruthi Mukund, Rohini Srihari, and Erik Peterson. 2010. An information-extraction system for urdu—a resource-poor language. *ACM Transactions on Asian Language Information Processing*, 9:15:1–15:43.

Iadh Ounis, Gianni Amati, Vassilis Plachouras, Ben He, Craig Macdonald, and Christina Lioma. 2006. Terrier: A High Performance and Scalable Information Retrieval Platform. In *Proceedings of ACM SIGIR'06 Workshop on Open Source Information Retrieval*, Seattle, WA, USA.

Martin F. Porter. 1980. An algorithm for suffix stripping. *Program*, 14(3):130–137.

Hema Raghavan and James Allan. 2004. Using soundex codes for indexing names in ASR documents. In *Proceedings of the HLT-NAACL 2004 Workshop on Interdisciplinary Approaches to Speech Indexing and Retrieval*, pages 22–27, Boston, MA.

Kashif Riaz. 2008. Baseline for Urdu IR evaluation. In *Proceeding of the 2nd ACM workshop on Improving non-English web searching*, pages 97–100, Napa, CA, USA.

Hassan Sajjad and Helmut Schmid. 2009. Tagging Urdu text with parts of speech: A tagger comparison. In *Proceedings of the 12th Conference of the European Chapter of the ACL*, pages 692–700, Athens, Greece.

Falk Scholer and Andrew Turpin. 2009. Metric and relevance mismatch in retrieval evaluation. In *Information Retrieval Technology*, volume 5839 of *Lecture Notes in Computer Science*, pages 50–62. Springer.

Prayut Suwanvisat and Somboon Prasitjutrakul. 1998. Thai-English cross-language transliterated word retrieval using soundex technique. In *Proceesings of the National Computer Science and Engineering Conference*, Bangkok, Thailand.

Unsupervised Russian POS Tagging with Appropriate Context

Li Yang, Erik Peterson, John Chen, Yana Petrova, and Rohini Srihari
Janya Inc.
1408 Sweet Home Road, Suite 1
Amherst, NY 14228, USA
lyang,epeterson,jchen,ypetrova,rohini@janya.com

Abstract

While adopting the contextualized hidden Markov model (CHMM) framework for unsupervised Russian POS tagging, we investigate the possibility of utilizing the left, right, and unambiguous context in the CHMM framework. We propose a backoff smoothing method that incorporates all three types of context into the transition probability estimation during the expectation-maximization process. The resulting model with this new method achieves overall and disambiguation accuracies comparable to a CHMM using the classic backoff smoothing method for HMM-based POS tagging from (Thede and Harper, 1999).

1 Introduction

A careful review of the work on unsupervised POS tagging in the past two decades reveals that the hidden Markov model (HMM) has been the standard approach since the seminal work of (Kupiec, 1992) and (Merialdo, 1994) and that researchers sought to improve HMM-based unsupervised POS tagging from a variety of perspectives, including exploring dictionary usage, context utilization, sparsity control and modeling, and parameter and model updates tuned to linguistic features. For example, (Banko and Moore, 2004) and (Goldberg et al., 2008) utilized contextualized HMM (CHMM) to capture rich context. To account for sparsity, (Goldwater and Griffiths, 2007) and (Johnson, 2007) utilized the Dirichlet hyperparameters of the Bayesian HMM. (Berg-Kirkpatrick et al., 2010) integrated the discriminative logistic regression model into the M-step of the standard generative model to allow rich linguistically-motivated features.

Unsupervised systems went beyond the mainstream HMM framework by employing methods such as prototype-driven clustering (Haghighi and Klein, 2006; Abend et al., 2010), Bayesian LDA (Toutanova and Johnson, 2007), integer programming (Ravi and Knight, 2009), and K-means clustering (Lamar et al., 2010).

Despite this large body of work, little effort has been devoted to unsupervised Russian POS tagging. Supervised Russian POS systems emerged in recent years. For example, eleven supervised systems entered the POS track of the 2010 Russian Morphological Parsers Evaluation [1]. Although the top two systems from the 2010 Evaluation achieved near perfect accuracy over the Russian National Corpus, little has been done on unsupervised Russian POS tagging. In this paper, we present our solution to unsupervised Russian POS tagging by adopting the CHMM. Our choice is based on the accuracy and efficiency of CHMM, an identical rationale to that behind (Goldberg et al., 2008).

We aim to achieve two goals. First, we intend to resolve the potential issue of missing useful contextual features by the backoff smoothing scheme in (Thede and Harper, 1999) and (Goldberg et al., 2008) for transition probabilities. Second, we explore the possibility of incorporating unambiguous context into transition probability estimation in an HMM framework. We propose a novel plan to achieve both goals in a unified approach.

In the following, we adopt the CHMM for unsupervised Russian POS tagging in section 2. Section 3 highlights the potential issue of missing useful left context in the backoff scheme by (Thede and Harper, 1999). Section 4 illustrates an updated backoff scheme to resolve this potential issue. This scheme also unifies the left, right, and unambiguous context. The experiments and discussion are presented in section 5. We present conclusions in section 6.

[1] See http://ru-eval.ru/tables_index.html

Proceedings of the 5th International Joint Conference on Natural Language Processing, pages 30–34,
Chiang Mai, Thailand, November 8-12, 2011.

2 CHMM for Russian POS Tagging

Our system is built upon the architecture of a contextualized HMM. Like other existing unsupervised HMM-based POS systems, the task of unsupervised POS tagging for us is to construct an HMM to predict the most likely POS tag sequence in the new data, given only a dictionary listing all possible parts-of-speech of a set of words and a large amount of unlabeled text for training.

Traditionally, the transition probability in a second-orderHMMis given by $p(t_i|t_{i-2}t_{i-1})$, and the emission probability by$p(w_i|t_i)$ ((Kriouile, 1990; Banko and Moore, 2004)). The CHMM, such as such as (Banko and Moore, 2004), (Adler, 2007), and (Goldberg et al., 2008),, incorporates more context into the transition and emission probabilities. Here, we adopt the transition probability p(ti—ti1ti+1) of (Adler, 2007) and (Goldberg et al., 2008) and the emission probability p(wi—titi+1) of (Adler, 2007).

Our training corpus consists of all 406,342 words of the plain text for training from the Appen Russian Named Entity Corpus [2], containing textual documents from a variety of sources. We created a POS dictionary for all 61,020 unique tokens in this corpus, using the output from the Russian lemmatizer [3]. The lemmatizer returns the stems of words and a list of POS tags for each word, relying on the morphology dictionary of the AOT Team [4]. Our tag set consists of 17 tags, comparable to those [5] used in Russian National Corpus (RNC), with the only addition of the Punct tag for punctuation marks. We relied on the Appen data because we did not have access to the RNC when our project was being developed. But we hope to be able to train and test out system with the RNC in the future.

3 Parameter Estimation and a Potential Issue

Given the model and resources for training described in section 2, we estimate the model parameters for our CHMM by following the standard EM procedures. During pre-processing, the dictionary is consulted, and a list of potential POS tags is provided for each word/token in the training sequence. In case of unknown words, the morphology analyzer built in the Russian lemmatizer suggests a list of tags. If the morphology analyzer does not make any suggestion, a list of open POS tags are assigned to the unknown words.

The potential POS tags in the training data provide counts to roughly esitimate the initial transition and emission probabilities. (Adler, 2007) initialized transition probabilities using a small portion of the training data. In our work, we initialize the emission probabilities using 20% of the training data with $p(w_i|t_it_{i+1}) = \frac{\#(w_i,t_i,t_{i+1})}{\#(t_i,t_{i+1})}$. During the EM process, we use additive smoothing when estimating $p(w_i|t_it_{i+1})$ (Chen, 1996).

We initialize the transition probabilities $p(t_i|t_{i-1}t_{i+1})$ with a uniform distribution. When re-estimating $p(t_i|t_{i-1}t_{i+1})$, we use the method from (Thede and Harper, 1999) for backoff smoothing in equation (1).

$$\hat{p}(t_i|t_{i-1}t_{i+1}) = \lambda_3\frac{N_3}{C_2} + (1-\lambda_3)\lambda_2 \cdot \frac{N_2}{C_1} + (1-\lambda_3)(1-\lambda_2)\cdot\frac{N_1}{C_0} \quad (1)$$

The λ coefficients are calculated the same way as in (Thede and Harper, 1999), that is $\lambda_2 = \frac{\log(N_2+1)+1}{\log(N_2+2)}$ and $\lambda_3 = \frac{\log(N_3+1)+1}{\log(N_3+2)}$. The counts, N_i and C_j are modified for our unsupervised CHMM, as shown in Table 1. Note that N_2 captures the counts of the bi-gram t_it_{i+1}, consisting of the current state t_i and its right context t_{i+1}.

(Thede and Harper, 1999) and (Goldberg et al., 2008) show that equation (1) is quite effective in both supervised and unsupervised scenarios. However, in our case where Russian is concerned, there are situations where equation (1) may not give good estimates.

Through RNC's online search tool, we discovered that the word from a specific set of pronouns following the comma is always analyzed as a conjunction, which itself can be followed by a number of possible POS tags. This set includes ambiguous words such as *chto* and *chem*. Although the Appen corpus does not come with POS tags, our Russian linguist observed similar linguistic regularties in the corpus. Some examples regarding *chto* from

$N_1 = N_1^e$	estimated counts of t_{i+1}
$N_2 = N_2^e$	estimated counts of t_it_{i+1}
$N_3 = N_3^e$	estimated counts of $t_{i-1}t_it_{i+1}$
$C_0 = C_0^e$	estimated total # of tags
$C_1 = C_1^e$	estimated counts of t_i
$C_2 = C_2^e$	estimated counts of $t_{i-1}t_{i+1}$

Table 1: Estimated counts as superscript ^{e}.

[2]Licensed from http://www.appen.com.au/
[3]Available at http://lemmatizer.org/en/
[4]See http://aot.ru/
[5]Listed at http://www.ruscorpora.ru

Appen are listed below.

Example 1 *,(Punct) chto(CONJ) na(PREP)*

Gloss comma and/or/that on

Example 2 *,(Punct) chto(CONJ) gotovy(ADJ)*

Gloss comma and/or/that ready

In the preceding examples, the comma to the left of chto provides for a useful clue. However, a potential issue arises when we estimate p(ti-1titi+1) using equation (1). That is, when the tri-gram $t_{i-1}t_it_{i+1}$ is rare and the first term of the equation is very small, the second term will affect $\hat{p}(t_{i-1}t_it_{i+1})$ more. The count, N_2, in the second term is for the bi-gram (*chto-CONJ, right word-POS*), right word-POS) but not for (*left word-comma, chto-CONJ*). Therefore, the useful clue in the latter bi-gram is missed. To resolve this, one cannot simply switch to the left context in N_2 because there are cases where the right context provides more of a clue. For example, observed from the Russian National Corpus, adjectival pronouns are only followed by a noun or an adjective and a noun, where the right context of adjectival pronouns are more important for disambiguating the adjectival pronouns. Several more examples from the Appen data where the left or right context contributing to disambiguation are listed in the Appendix.

4 Incorporating All Three Types of Context

Several systems made use of the information provided in unambiguous POS tag sequence. (Brill, 1995) learned rules from the context of unambiguous words. (Mihalcea, 2003) created equivalence classes from unambiguous words for training. We expected the assumption that unambiguous context helps with disambiguation to hold for Russian as well.

$N_1 = N_1^u$, # of unambiguous counts of t_{i+1}
$N_2^L = N_2^{uL}$, # of unamb. bi-gram $t_{i-1}t_i$ w left context t_{i-1}
$N_2^R = N_2^{uR}$, # of unamb. bi-gram t_it_{i+1} w right context t_{i+1}
$N_3 = N_3^u$, # of unamb. tri-gram $t_{i-1}t_it_{i+1}$
$C_0 = C_0^u$, total # of unamb. tags
$C_1 = C_1^u$, # of unamb. t_i
$C_2 = C_2^u$, # of unamb. bi-gram of $t_{i-1}t_{i+1}$

Table 2: Counts of unambiguous tri-grams, bi-grams, and unigrams. The superscript ^{u} stands for unambiguous counts.

$N_1^u \leftarrow N_1^e$	estimated counts of t_{i+1}
$N_2^{uL} \leftarrow N_2^{eL}$	estimated counts of $t_{i-1}t_i$
$N_2^{uR} \leftarrow N_2^{eR}$	estimated counts of t_it_{i+1}
$N_3^u \leftarrow N_3^e$	estimated counts of $t_{i-1}t_it_{i+1}$
$C_0^u \leftarrow C_0^e$	estimated total # of tags
$C_1^u \leftarrow C_1^e$	estimated counts of t_i
$C_2^u \leftarrow C_2^e$	estimated counts of $t_{i-1}t_{i+1}$

Table 3: Replacement plan for unambiguous counts

In the Appen training corpus, 84% of the words/tokens have a unique POS tag, based on our dictionary and the Russian lemmatizer. We can easily spot examples in the corpus where unambiguous context helps with disambiguation. Again, in our earlier example, *,(Punct) chto(CONJ) na(PREP)*, the unambiguous left context ',' reveals that *chto* is a CONJ instead of a PRON. To take advantage of the unambiguous context, we collect the counts for all unambiguous tri-gram and bi-gram sequences in the Appen training corpus and integrate these counts into equation (2) through the equivalence in Table 2.

$$\begin{aligned}\hat{p}(t_i|t_{i-1}t_{i+1}) &= \lambda_3\frac{N_3}{C_2} \\ &+(1-\lambda_3)\lambda_2\cdot\frac{N_2^L}{C_1^L}\times\frac{N_2^R}{C_1^R} \\ &+(1-\lambda_3)(1-\lambda_2)\cdot\frac{N_1}{C_0} \quad (2)\end{aligned}$$

where $\lambda_2 = \frac{\log(N_2^L+1)+1}{\log(N_2^L+2)} \times \frac{\log(N_2^R+1)+1}{\log(N_2^R+2)}$, and $\lambda_3 = \frac{\log(N_3+1)+1}{\log(N_3+2)}$. λ_2 incorporates both the left and right context. The unambiguous counts are defined in Table 2.

Now that the new backoff smoothing plan combines both the left and right unambiguous bi-gram counts, we extend this plan to cover the cases where the unambiguous tri/bi/uni-grams are not available, by replacing them with the estimated counts from Table 1. Table 3 displays the scheme for replacing an unambiguous count with an estimated count from the EM process.

5 Experiments and Results

We designed three experiments to test three combinations of the context, in addition to experimenting with a traditional second-order HMM. The Appen corpus contains a development set and an

Model & setting(s)	Overall Accuracy	Disamb. Accuracy
2nd-order HMM	94.88%	63.42%
CHMM_left_context	95.72%	69.42%
CHMM_right_context	96.05%	71.78%
CHMM_unique_ ← _left/right context	96.06%	71.85%

Table 4: Experiments, overall and disambiguation accuracies over test data

evaluation set. We passed both sets through the Russian lemmatizer to obtain POS tags for the data and had the tags manually corrected by a Russian linguist. Thus, we have created both development and evaluation data. 14% of words/tokens in both development and evaluation data have multiple POS tags. Table 4 summarizes our experimental settings and results over the evaluation data.

The second-order HMM was trained with the traditional transition probability $p(t_i|t_{i-2}t_{i-1})$ and emission probability $p(w_i|t_i)$. It gained an overall accuracy of 94.88%, and was able to correctly disambiguate 63.42% of the ambiguous words/tokens.

All three CHMM models were trained with the emission probability $p(w_i|t_i t_{i+1})$ initialized with 20% of the unlabeled training corpus. Model *CHMM_left_context* considered the left context bi-gram $t_{i-1}t_i$ when calculating the second term in equation (1). Model *CHMM_right_context* considered the right context bi-gram $t_i t_{i+1}$ when calculating the same term. Model *CHMM_unique_ ← _left/right* unified both unambiguous context counts and estimated counts for left and right context from the EM process, using equation (2).

All CHMM models achieved accuracies 1% higher than the HMM, while the disambiguation accuracies from the former three are $7-9\%$ higher than the latter. This shows that the CHMM models capture more useful context information for Russian POS tagging than the traditional HMM. At the same time, the overall and disambiguation accuracies between *CHMM_right_context* and *CHMM_unique_ ← _left/right* are comparable. Error analyses indicate that a backoff scheme for emission probabilities is also needed to incorporate the left context.

6 Conclusion and Future Work

We adopted the CHMM to unsupervised Russian POS tagging. The CHMM models using either the left or right context were able to outperform the traditional second-order HMM. To resolve the potential issue of missing out the left context with the classic smoothing scheme in (Thede and Harper, 1999), we experimented with an approach to unifying the information provided in the left, right, and unambiguous contexts. The results from the latter were comparable to a CHMM with the classic backoff smoothing method in (Thede and Harper, 1999), although we expected a more significant improvement. We plan to investigate a backoff scheme for emission probabilities where we will incorporate the left context as well, while currently we only rely on additive smoothing for emission probabilities.

Acknowledgments

We would like to thank the anonymous reviewers for their valuable comments and suggestions. Our work was partially funded by the Air Force Research Laboratory/RIEH in Rome, New York through contracts FA8750-09-C-0038 and FA8750-10-C-0124.

References

Omri Abend, Roi Reichart, and Ari Rappoport. 2010. Improved unsupervised pos induction through prototype discovery. In *Proceedings of the 48th ACL.*

Meni Adler. 2007. *Hebrew Morphological Disambiguation.* Ph.D. thesis, University of the Negev.

Michele Banko and Robert C. Moore. 2004. Part of speech tagging in context. In *Proceedings of the 20th international conference on Computational Linguistics.*

Taylor Berg-Kirkpatrick, Alexandre Bouchard-Ct, John DeNero, and Dan Klein. 2010. Painless unsupervised learning with features. In *Proceedings of NAACL 2010.*

Eric Brill, 1995. *Very Large*, chapter Unsupervised Learning of Disambiguation Rules for Part of Speech Tagging, pages 1–13. Kluwer Academic Press.

Stanley F. Chen. 1996. *Building Probabilistic Models for Natural Language.* Ph.D. thesis, Harvard University.

Yoav Goldberg, Meni Adler, and Michael Elhadad. 2008. Em can find pretty good pos taggers (when given a good start). In *Proceedings of ACL-08: HLT.*

Sharon Goldwater and Tom Griffiths. 2007. A fully bayesian approach to unsupervised part-of-speech tagging. In *Proceedings of the 45th ACL.*

Aria Haghighi and Dan Klein. 2006. Prototype-driven learning for sequence models. In *Proceedings of the main conference on HLT-NAACL.*

Mark Johnson. 2007. Why doesnt em find good hmm pos-taggers. In *n EMNLP*.

Abdelaziz Kriouile. 1990. Some improvements in speech recognition algorithms based on hmm. In *Acoustics, Speech, and Signal Processing*.

Julian Kupiec. 1992. Robust part-of-speech tagging using a hidden markov model. *Computer Speech & Language*, 6:225–242.

Michael Lamar, Yariv Maron, and Elie Bienenstock. 2010. Latent descriptor clustering for unsupervised pos induction. In *EMNLP 2010*.

Bernard Merialdo. 1994. Tagging english text with a probabilistic model. *Computational Linguistics*, 20:155–171.

Rada Mihalcea. 2003. The role of non-ambiguous words in natural language disambiguation. In *Proceedings of the Conference on RANLP*.

Sujith Ravi and Kevin Knight. 2009. Minimized models for unsupervised part-of-speech tagging. In *Proceedings of ACL-IJCNLP 2009,*, pages 504–512.

Scott M. Thede and Mary P. Harper. 1999. A second-order hidden markov model for part-of-speech tagging. In *Proceedings of the 37th Annual Meeting of the ACL*.

Kristina Toutanova and Mark Johnson. 2007. A bayesian lda-based model for semi-supervised part-of-speech tagging. In *Proceedings of NIPS*.

Appendix: Linguistic Patterns Observed in Appen

In Section 3, we illustrated how the left context helped to disambiguate *chto*. In the following we present several more examples from the Appen corpus illustrating the helpful left or right context. While the patterns our Russian linguist observed are common in both the RNC and Appen, the counts and statistics regarding each pattern are unavailable for reporting because the RNC was then inaccessible to us and Appen was not tagged with POS tags.

Examples 3 through 7 show that the left context of *chem*, *poka*, and *kak* helps to disambiguate them as conjuctions.

Example 3 *,(Punct) chem(CONJ) v(PREP) stolitse(NOUN)*

Gloss comma and/than in capital

Example 4 *,(Punct) poka(CONJ) eta(PRONOUN)*

Gloss comma yet this

Example 5 *,(Punct) poka(CONJ) Sovet(NOUN)*

Gloss comma yet council

Example 6 *,(Punct) kak(CONJ) dva(NUMERAL) neudachnika(NOUN)*

Gloss comma as two losers

Example 7 *,(Punct) kak(CONJ) on(PRONOUN)*

Gloss comma as he

The next examples show that the right context determines the adjectival tag, *PRONOUN_P*, of the pronouns.

Example 8 *obekty(NOUN) svoey(PRONOUN_P) sistemy(NOUN)*

Gloss units their/they system

Example 9 *esli(CONJ) mnogie(PRONOUN_P) mnogie(NOUN)*

Gloss if many/various emigrants

Extending a multilingual Lexical Resource by bootstrapping Named Entity Classification using Wikipedia's Category System

Johannes Knopp
KR & KM Research Group, Department of Computer Science
Universität Mannheim, B6 26, 68159 Mannheim, Germany
johannes@informatik.uni-mannheim.de

Abstract

Named Entity Recognition and Classification (NERC) is a well-studied NLP task which is typically approached using machine learning algorithms that rely on training data whose creation usually is expensive. The high costs result in the lack of NERC training data for many languages. An approach to create a multilingual NE corpus was presented in Wentland et al. (2008). The resulting resource called *HeiNER* describes a valuable number of NEs but does not include their types. We present a bootstrap approach based on Wikipedia's category system to classify the NEs contained in HeiNER that is able to classify more than two million named entities to improve the resource's quality.

1 Introduction

For tasks in information extraction NERC is very important and often supervised machine learning approaches are used to solve it, e.g. Bender et al. (2003) or Szarvas et al. (2006). In *A survey of named entity recognition and classification* David Nadeau and Satoshi Sekine conclude:

> "When supervised learning is used, a prerequisite is the availability of a large collection of annotated data. Such collections are available from the evaluation forums but remain rather rare and limited in domain and language coverage" (Nadeau and Sekine, 2007)

To overcome the problem of limited language coverage, Wentland et al. (2008) started to create the multilingual *Heidelberg Named Entity Resource (HeiNER)*. In more than 250 languages, HeiNER lists Wikipedia (WP) articles that describe a named entity (NE), in 16 of those languages it contains a collection of textual contexts a NE was unambigiously mentioned in. Those contexts provide useful training material for NE classification, thus the goal of this work is to add NE types to HeiNER's entries.

Unlike the widely used machine learning approaches to NERC our classification method relies only on WP's category system and thus does not need any language specific information. The idea is to first determine sets of WP categories to identify each NE type. After that, these sets are used to initialize a bootstrapping algorithm that identifies the types for unclassified NEs. NE types follow the CoNLL definition presented by Sang (2002): person (PER), location (LOC), organization (ORG) and miscellaneous (MISC).[1] The CoNLL types were chosen because HeiNER's evaluation was based on the CoNLL types.

The following sections reveal details about HeiNER (section 2), describe the bootstrap approach of NE classification with WP categories (section 3) and show the results in the evaluation section (section 4).

2 HeiNER

As this work builds upon the Heidelberg Named Entity Resource (HeiNER), we will describe the data that HeiNER provides and how they were created to give the reader an idea about their quality and structure.

HeiNER is a multilingual collection of *named entities* along with *disambiguated context excerpts* and a *disambiguation dictionary* that maps proper names to a set of NEs the proper names may refer to. The resource was created automatically from Wikipedia relying on (i) the heuristic presented in Bunescu and Paşca (2006) to recognize English Wikipedia articles that denote a NE and (ii) Wikipedia's link structure.

[1] cf. http://www.cnts.ua.ac.be/conll2003/ner/annotation.txt

Proceedings of the 5th International Joint Conference on Natural Language Processing, pages 35–43,
Chiang Mai, Thailand, November 8-12, 2011.

```
<transDict>
<namedEntity id='2134'>
<an>Organización d'as Nazions Unitas</an>
<bs>Ujedinjeni narodi</bs>
<ga>Nisiin Aontaithe</ga>
<gl>ONU</gl>
<hu>Egyesült Nemzetek Szervezete</hu>
<lb>Vereent Natiounen</lb>
<nds>Vereente Natschonen</nds>
<tr>Birleşmiş Milletler</tr>
<en>United Nations</en>
...
</namedEntity>
</transDict>
```

Figure 1: Example of the entry for "United Nations" in the translation dictionary

First, the NER heuristic based on uppercase letters generated a list of English WP articles that denote a NE. This method created more than 1.5 million NEs with a precision of 95% [2]. With help of WP's interlanguage links the available translations for every NE were added to the list resulting in the *translation dictionary* shown in figure 1. All of the more than 250 languages available in WP were considered to create the NE translations.

As the NE articles in WP are known from the first step, the disambiguation dictionary is built afterwards using disambiguation and redirect links to map proper names to NEs. Finally the context dataset is created for every NE by storing the paragraphs they are unambiguously mentioned in. This was done for 16 languages. An excerpt of the context dataset is shown in Figure 2 below.

```
<dataset  neID='2134' lang='en'
          neStr='United Nations'>
<context id='0'>
 <surfaceForm>United Nations</surfaceForm>
 <leftContext>
 The World Health Organization (WHO) is a
 specialized agency of the
 </leftContext>
 <rightContext>
 (UN) that acts as a coordinating
 authority on international public health.
 </rightContext>
</context>
</dataset>
```

Figure 2: Excerpt from the English context dataset for the NE "United Nations"

The NEs together with disambiguated contexts in different languages can be considered useful data for NE disambiguation, classification or machine translation (e.g. Federmann and Hunsicker (2011)).[3] For this paper the heuristics to create the list of English NEs were run on the more recent WP dump of November 3rd 2009 and resulted in a total of 2,225,193 found NEs compared to 1,547,586 NEs reported in the original paper. The difference is solely caused by the natural growth of Wikipedia.

3 A Bootstrap Approach to NE Classification with WP Categories

As described in Section 2 HeiNER presents a lot of context information of NEs. To release the full potential of the multilingual data the NEs need to be annotated with their respective type.

Instead of using a classical NER system this work concentrates on a language agnostic approach that is based on WP's category structure which is not only suited for NER but can be used for other classifications based on WP categories as well. In short, the idea is to identify WP categories that correspond to a NE type and then use those categories to classify NEs that are placed in those *typed categories*. The categories can be interpreted as a signature or footprint of a NE type. The method outline is as follows: First, for every NE type a list of seed categories is created manually. It is enhanced by taking two levels of subcategories into account. The resulting lists of type specific categories are used to classify the articles in HeiNER by looking up if they are placed in one of the seed categories and assigning the respective type. The steps are illustrated in figure 3.

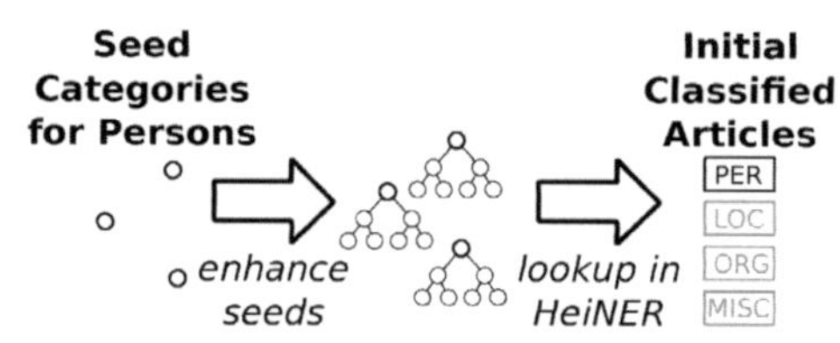

Figure 3: The manually chosen and enhanced seed categories generate the initial list of classified articles. The illustration shows the method for PER, it works in the same way for the other categories.

This leaves most of the NEs in HeiNER unclassified, but the initially classified NEs can be used for the bootstrapping solution that is visualized in figure 4: For every NE type, a NE type vector

[2]Read Wentland et al. (2008) for more details.

[3]HeiNER is available for the scientific community at http://heiner.cl.uni-heidelberg.de/

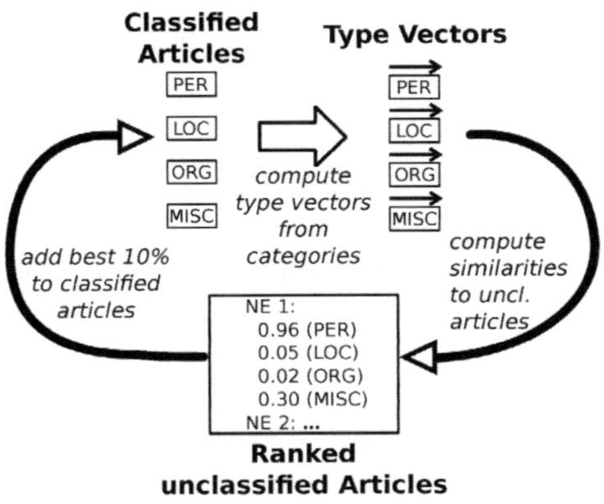

Figure 4: Bootstrapping loop to classify articles.

based on categories is built by looking up all categories of the now classified articles and counting them for each type. The articles are then classified by computing the similarity between their category vector and the four NE type vectors and choosing the most similar one. This is done in ten iterations where each step updates the type vectors with the new classified articles. The only manual work needed is collecting the seed categories. This can be applied in any language that is available in WP. We use the English version because it is by far the largest edition. Also note that the seeds define the result of the classification. More fine grained types like *politician* or *entertainer* (cf. (Fleischman and Hovy, 2002)) could be easily implemented by choosing other seeds.

After this broad overview the subsections present a more detailed description of the approach. For that we introduce the notation scheme used in this paper:

The set of NE types $t \in T$ consists of persons PER, locations LOC, organizations ORG and miscellaneous $MISC$.

C denotes the set of all categories in the English Wikipedia. Single Categories that are mentioned in the text are written in SMALL CAPS.

3.1 Generating Seed Categories

For every NE type the seed categories hold a set of WP categories such that any NE article that is placed in one of them is considered to be of the type the category is associated with. Because the classification method relies on the seeds' quality they have to be annotated manually. The goal is to find categories that are broad enough to classify as many NEs as possible but also are accurate in order to avoid incorrect classifications.

To find the best seed categories for the NE types person, location, organization and miscellaneous, we started to randomly pick NE articles belonging to one type, then inspect the categories it is placed in and move up in the category tree by following supercategories until the topic range of a category gets too broad for unambiguous classification. The broad-but-accurate categories are added to the seed set of the respective type. Because the subcategories can be considered to be useful for the classification process, we add two levels of subcategories to the initial seed list. The restriction to two levels of subcategories is needed to avoid adding noise, because WP's category system is a graph, not a tree.

An example for the manual creation of seed categories might help at this point: if we are interested in the NE type person, we start with a random WP article about a person, e.g. Jimmy Hendrix. We always follow the most promising supercategories which leads to the following chain:
1960S SINGERS ⇒ SINGERS BY TIME PERIOD ⇒ PEOPLE BY OCCUPATION AND PERIOD ⇒ PEOPLE BY OCCUPATION ⇒ PEOPLE

The accuracy of each category is checked by inspecting subcategories and articles belonging to it. The category PEOPLE has a subcategory BIBLIOGRAPHY which deals with biographical books. Thus, PEOPLE itself is not accurate enough to find persons. Still most of the subcategories of PEOPLE like PEOPLE BY OCCUPATION or PEOPLE BY RELIGION are added to the seed categories of NE type person.

As a result there are 15 seed categories found for the type person. The same was carried out for the other NE types. All seed categories together with two levels of subcategories form the set of typed categories C_t. The results can be seen in table 1.

The number of seed categories does not necessarily correlate with the number of found subcategories: The types PER and LOC have the same count of seed categories, but C_{PER} is almost 3.5 times bigger than C_{LOC} and has about 1,500 categories more than C_{ORG} which started with 75 seed categories. An explanation would be that persons are supported well and have a very fine grained categorization while locations can be described with a smaller set of categories. C_{MISC} remains in between the others with 4,747 subcategories.

type t	seed categories	sub-categories	typed categories C_t
PER	15	9,625	9,640
LOC	15	2,783	2,798
ORG	75	8,033	8,108
MISC	27	4,747	4,774

Table 1: Numbers of categories found for each NE type derived from seed categories.

3.2 Initial Named Entity Classification

Starting from the enhanced seed categories the initial list of classified NEs can be created easily. Just iterate over every article in HeiNER and check if it is placed in C_t. If this is the case the article can be considered to be of type t and hence is added to the set of classified NE articles NE_t. If more than one type was found for an article it is left unclassified. The results of this initial classification are shown in table 2.

To point out the generative power of the categories the last row shows the "productivity ratio" $\frac{NE_t}{C_t}$ of each category. The earlier assumption that there are more articles of type PER than others is supported by the fact that more than half million NEs could be initially classified and also by the number of articles found per category. This cannot be solely based on the superior count of PER categories because the number of ORG related categories is not that far behind, though NE_{ORG} is about 4 times smaller than NE_{PER}. Also the PER related categories are about five times more productive than the ones related to MISC. In other words, most of WP's contributors write articles about NEs of the type PER and categorize them studiously. The quality of the results will be discussed in the evaluation in section 4.

Type t	C_t	NE_t	$\frac{NE_t}{C_t}$
PER	9,640	502,173	52
LOC	2,798	41,539	15
ORG	8,108	128,433	16
MISC	4,774	47,887	10

Table 2: Number of classified articles derived from seed categories. The last row shows the rounded average classification produced by each category.

3.3 Type Vectors & Bootstrapping

After the initial classification step we can remove the 720,032 classified articles from the NE list with 2,224,472 entries leaving 1,504,440 yet to classify articles. As the presented method relies on categories 7,033 articles without any categorization are removed too which results in a final list of 1,497,407 NEs that need to be classified in the bootstrapping process.

As explained earlier the categories of the classified articles are used to build a NE type vector consisting of categories associated with NEs of a certain type. The categories of classified articles form the dimensions of the type vectors, their counts define the length in that dimension. The algorithm in figure 5 shows how the vector is created. Note that for the NE type vector all categories are taken into account and not just the ones pointing to NEs that were used in the initial classification step. The intuition behind this is that the aggregated categories form the footprint of a type even if not each of them points to a NE.

```
def compute_vector(NE_t):
  #store vector as a dictionary
  category_vector = {}
  for article in NE_t:
    for c in article.catgories:
      if category_vector.has_key(c):
        category_vector[c] += 1
      else:
        category_vector[c] = 1
  return category_vector
```

Figure 5: Python-Pseudocode algorithm of a function to build the category vector. The vector is stored in a dictionary where the category name is the key and the count its value.

The algorithm is applied to each NE type in NE_t, the results are shown in table 3. The dimensions of the vectors in the third row show the number of unique categories. The fourth row represents the overall count of categories in the articles and the last row shows the average number of categories per article. Again we can see that PER is categorized in more detail while LOC and ORG have a similar ratio. MISC has the lowest categorization rate. We expect our method to work best with articles that are placed in many categories.

The type of an unclassified NE article is determined by converting its categories into a vector, computing similarities to the type vectors, and as-

type t	NE_t	dimen-sions	category count	categories per NE_t
PER	502,173	132,098	4,037,634	7.86
LOC	41,539	35,880	228,468	5.08
ORG	128,433	72,184	694,523	4.94
MISC	47,887	33,110	229,438	4.33

Table 3: Statistics for the NE type vectors that are created for NE_t.

signing the type with the highest similarity score. As categories can either be present or not the category vector of an article is binary. In order to verify the general approach we classify the NEs in two setups using different similarity measures, *cosine similarity* and *Dice's coefficient*:

$$cosine(\vec{x}, \vec{y}) = \frac{\sum_{k=1}^{n} x_k y_k}{\sqrt{\sum_{k=1}^{n} x_k^2} \cdot \sqrt{\sum_{k=1}^{n} y_k^2}}$$

$$dice(\vec{x}, \vec{y}) = \frac{2 \cdot \sum_{k=1}^{n} (weight_{xk} \cdot weight_{yk})}{\sum_{k=1}^{n} weight_{xk} + \sum_{k=1}^{n} weight_{yk}}$$

Cosine similarity computes the angle between the two vectors taking only the directions of type vectors into account and not their length. Because there are no negative categorizations the resulting similarities range between zero and one. The Dice's coefficient includes the count of shared elements in relation to all elements that are not zero. It considers the weights of the vectors by multiplying the shared elements[4]. The factor 2 keeps the result range between zero and one.

In the bootstrapping phase HeiNER's unclassified NEs are classified as just described. In 10 iterations the 10% with the highest similarity values are added to their respective set NE_t and the type vectors are updated before the next 10% are classified. Figure 6 shows the process for cosine similarity and figure 7 for Dice's coefficient.

For each NE type the tables list the exact counts of how many NEs were added in each of the 10 iterations. The bar plots beneath the tables visualize these data by stacking the counts of each type in every iteration. As the sum is always 10% of the initially unclassified data the bars have the same length. The exception at iteration 10 stems from the fact that articles that do not share a category with any of the type vectors cannot be classified. The difference between the last Dice and cosine bar is a result of the different classification decisions made in the bootstrapping process.

Inspecting the results we can see that the lion's share in the first iteration in both setups is classified as LOC. This indicates that many locations were missed by the enhanced seed categories, but the type vector allowed to find the missed NEs. Following iterations do not show a bias towards LOC which supports this analysis. Nevertheless cosine similarity seems to be biased towards MISC because on average about 60,000 articles are added to this type per iteration resulting in the biggest gain in 8 of the 10 iterations. This could be caused by cosine similarity's ignorance of weights in the type vector thus preferring articles that share

run	PER	LOC	ORG	MISC
initial	**502,173**	41,539	128,433	47,887
		Cosine		
1	3,999	**120,641**	23,469	1,631
2	1,216	11,456	42,997	**94,071**
3	1,414	**56,725**	38,220	53,381
4	33,664	11,763	39,064	**65,249**
5	50,990	10,690	17,511	**70,549**
6	44,166	24,131	22,569	**58,874**
7	14,924	39,565	33,347	**61,904**
8	4,482	45,417	37,201	**62,640**
9	3,392	38,138	38,711	**69,499**
10	4,057	26,395	38,719	**60,913**
Bootstrap	162,304	384,921	331,808	**598,711**
Total	**664,477**	426,460	460,241	646,598
Plus	32%	927%	258%	**1250%**

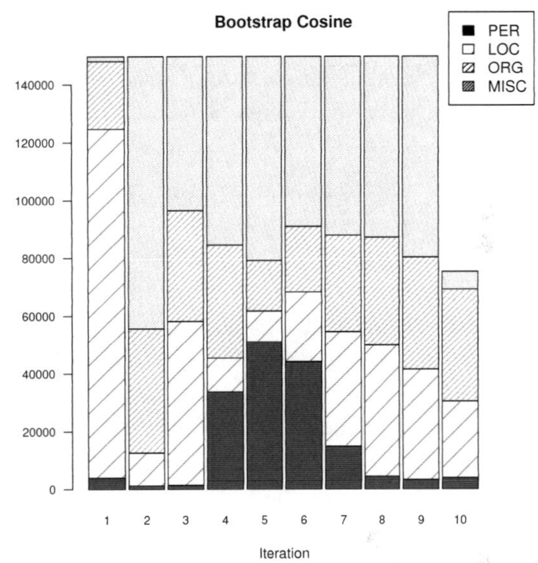

Figure 6: Bootstrapping using cosine similarity. The bar plot shows the visualization of the NE type classifications in the table above.

[4]As we multiply with a binary vector we just decide whether to add the value of the non-binary vector at that position or not.

many categories with a type vector over articles with less but higher weighted categories. MISC might have thematically wide spread categories supporting that effect. However, the bias towards that type cannot solely be based on this property, because the initialized vector is the one with the least dimensions in comparison to the others.

Bootstrapping using the Dice's coefficient tends to be biased towards LOC and ORG, the former showing an overall gain of 1,308 percent[5]. In four of the iterations ORG wins the majority of new classified articles, LOC is in advantage in five of the iterations leaving PER one major gain in the fifth run. Because Dice's coefficient takes the counts of categories into account, it is likely that the unclassified articles are placed in some of the categories that have high values for LOC and ORG.

The count of articles added to PER develops remarkably similar for both measures. They start with few new articles in the first three iterations, rise to many more additions in steps four, five and six to slow down again in the left iterations. In both cases eventually PER is the NE type with the least added articles (cf. lines "Bootstrap"), but still the biggest count when summing it up with the initial count (cf. lines "Total"). No other named entity type shows such a strong correlation between the two different similarity measures. This indicates that most of the articles were already classified in the initialization proving the seed categories for that type to be of high quality.

In summary, both bootstrapping setups are able to classify almost all of the unclassified NEs, but differ a lot in their results with the exception of the type PER.

4 Evaluation

Before the bootstrapping phase an evaluation set of NEs was created and excluded from the process. It consists of NEs of each type: 295 PER, 192 LOC, 110 ORG and 122 MISC entries that were annotated manually by one annotator. Both setups are evaluated by classifying the NEs in the same way as in the bootstrapping and investigating the precision of the results.

[5]This growth is narrowed a little bit by the fact that it started with the smallest count of articles.

run	PER	LOC	ORG	MISC
initial	**502,173**	41,539	128,433	47,887
Dice's coefficient				
1	5,271	**137,051**	6,406	1,012
2	17	25	**138,578**	11,120
3	1,266	58,780	**65,593**	24,101
4	36,595	16,952	**56,017**	40,176
5	**67,975**	31,508	25,819	24,438
6	38,196	**56,745**	45,219	9,580
7	16,166	**67,458**	54,813	11,303
8	8,969	**67,890**	52,944	19,937
9	5,581	**65,655**	46,860	31,644
10	5,751	41,301	**56,864**	26,323
Bootstrap	185,787	543,365	**549,113**	199,634
Total	**687,960**	584,904	677,546	247,521
Plus	37%	**1,308%**	427%	417%

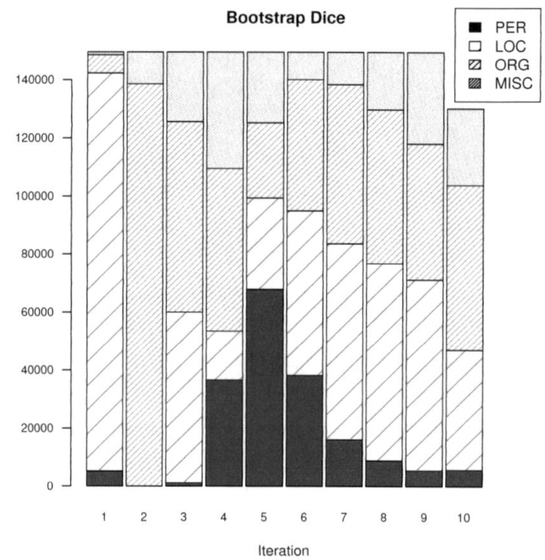

Figure 7: Bootstrapping using Dice's coefficient. The bar plot shows the visualization of the NE type classifications in the table above.

4.1 Initial type vectors

The confusion matrix in table 4 shows the results using the type vector from the initial NE classifications. The rate of correct classifications varies from 35.25% (MISC, Dice's coefficient) to 81.02% (PER, Dice's coefficient). It is not surprising that PER is the best performing named entity type when we remember the earlier statement that articles of that type are categorized with high detail and that this NE type has by far the highest count of instances after the initialization. This is underlined by the fact that almost no instances were classified incorrectly as a person in the other evaluation sets. Consequently, there is no much confusion between persons and other NE types.

Eval. set	PER	LOC	ORG	MISC	UNCL
Cosine					
PER (295)	78.64% (232)	5.76% (17)	8.47% (25)	6.44% (19)	0.68% (2)
LOC (192)	0.0% (0)	60.42% (116)	10.94% (21)	7.29% (14)	21.35% (41)
ORG (110)	0.91% (1)	15,45% (17)	**67.27% (74)**	8.18% (9)	8.18% (9)
MISC (122)	0.82% (1)	8.2% (10)	**38.52% (47)**	37.7% (46)	14.75% (18)
Dice's coefficient					
PER (295)	**81.02% (239)**	6.1% (18)	7.8% (23)	4.41% (13)	0.68% (2)
LOC (192)	0.0% (0)	**64.06% (123)**	9.9% (19)	4.69% (9)	21.35% (41)
ORG (110)	1.82% (2)	19.09% (21)	64.55% (71)	6.36% (7)	8.18% (9)
MISC (122)	3.28% (4)	9.84% (12)	36.89% (45)	35.25% (43)	14.75% (18)

Table 4: Confusion matrix for the CoNLL named entity types. Members of evaluation sets for every type were classified by computing similarities to the initialised named entity type vectors. The overall highest values (cosine and Dice similarity) are marked as boldface. The percentages show the fraction of the absolute numbers that are given in the first row, the numbers in braces show the absolute numbers.

Considering that 21.35% of the articles were left unclassified, only 18.23% (cosine) and 14.59% (Dice) of LOC were explicitly classified wrong. Unclassified articles occur if none of the instances in the evaluation set LOC has categories that can be found in any of the NE type vectors. This could either mean that the seed categories for this type were not chosen broad enough or that articles of type LOC are placed in categories that are wide spread over WP's category graph and cannot be grouped easily. The bootstrapping results indicated that the former case is more likely. ORG are classified correctly with a chance of 67.27% (cosine) and 64.55% (Dice) leaving an error rate of 24.55% (cosine) and 27.27% (Dice). Cosine outperforms the Dice's coefficient in this class.

The CoNLL definitions of MISC do not seem to correspond well with WP categories. For the evaluation set of type MISC more instances were classified as an organization in both setups. That indicates a high probability to confuse members of MISC with LOC which is not that surprising, recalling that the definition of this type is "words of which one part is a location, organization, miscellaneous or person"(Sang, 2002). Further investigation would be necessary to judge whether type overlaps are just caused by incorrect classifications or if the articles really do belong to that class and maybe should be allowed to be classified as both MISC and LOC. For example a book that has a location in its title like *The Restaurant at the End of the Universe* could benefit from a double classification because depending on the context it may serve as one or the other.

The results of the initialization step show that in general the MUC-6 named entity types(Grishman and Sundheim, 1996) PER, LOC and ORG can be classified with this approach reasonably well with 60.42% (LOC, cosine) as lower and 81.02% (PER, Dice) as an upper bound. This does not work out as well for MISC, but still the lower bound of 35.25% (Dice) beats a baseline with randomly assigned types that would result in 25% correct classifications. Thus, the initially constructed type vectors are useful for NEC of WP articles. At this time it is not possible to say which of the similarity measures returns better results.

4.2 Bootstrapping Iterations

To evaluate the iterative classification phase we used the resulting type vectors of every step to classify the evaluation set and again analyze the percentage of NEs that were classified correctly. [6]

Figure 8 shows the results per iteration for each type and setup. The continuous line represents cosine similarity while the dashed line represents Dice's coefficient. To see which setup works best compared to the other the different lines marked with the same symbols must be compared. The lines point out the development of the quality of the type vectors.

After every iteration the type vector is refined which should improve classifications. However, because every classification step only incorporates the best or most certain 10% of unclassified NEs leaving the less clear NEs unclassified, the preci-

[6] Because the annotated data represent only a fraction of the whole data we cannot provide reliable recall results.

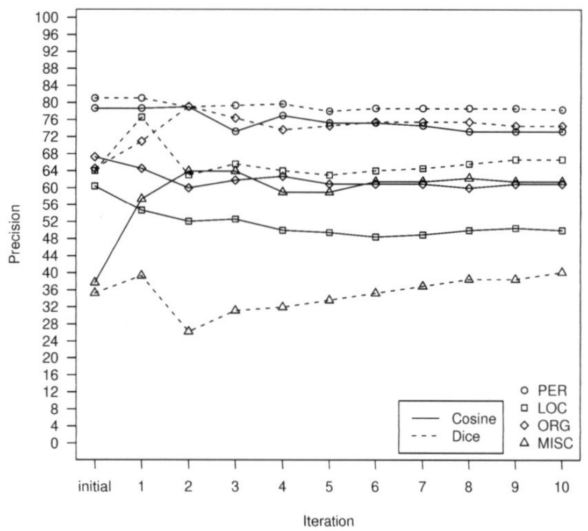

Figure 8: Precision of the classification for the iterations in the bootstrapping phase.

sion is expected to decrease in later iterations due to introduced noise. Thus a stable line indicates a successful approach.

If we ignore MISC for a moment, the cosine setup has an overall decrease in precision relative to their starting point while the Dice setup is fairly stable or even better. The difficulty of representing the MISC type with WP categories seems to be the reason for its different behaviour, the broad choice of categories creates the bias of the cosine method. Dice's coefficient is more robust and seems to avoid that noise making it more suitable for the task. This can be seen after the first iteration: As discussed in section 3.3 the biggest fraction was classified as LOC. While the precision of Dice's coefficient increases by more than 10% in this iteration the precision of the cosine setup drops more than 5% which implies that many NEs were classified wrong. Finally, the best results after bootstrapping are:

- *PER* – Dice 78.31% (cosine 73.22%)
- *LOC* – Dice 66.67% (cosine: 50%)
- *ORG* – Dice 74.55% (cosine: 60.91%)
- *MISC* – cosine 61.48% (Dice: 40.16%)

Dice coefficient performs better than cosine similarity for three out of four NE types, which implies that taking statistical evidence into account improves the performance of the classification. The numbers indicate that cosine similarity beats Dice coefficient at the classification of *Miscellaneous* because it is biased.

5 Conclusion

In this paper we have shown a language-agnostic method to classify more than two million NEs in the multilingual lexical resource HeiNER (Wentland et al., 2008) in two steps, adhering to the CoNLL definition of NEs (Sang, 2002; Sang and Meulder, 2003) relying on structural information only. First, we initialized 700,032 classified NEs utilizing the category system of Wikipedia starting with a set of 132 manually annotated seed categories. As the method relies only on WP's structure any classification task that can be represented by WP categories can be approached this way for any language available in WP. Second, the categories of these classified articles were used to create NE type vectors to classify yet unlabelled articles by computing the similarities between the vectors and unclassified articles' categories. This was done via bootstrapping in two setups that work with two similarity measures: cosine similarity and Dice's coefficient. The results were evaluated on manually annotated data and showed that the type vectors created from the initialization step easily outperform a random baseline and that the method is suited well for the NE types used in MUC-6 (Grishman and Sundheim, 1996) but that the additional CoNLL class MISC shows a gap in quality because it is harder to map the latter to Wikipedia categories. The evaluation of bootstrapping iterations reveals that Dice's coefficient is the better similarity measure for this particular task. This can be attributed to its property of taking the weights of the vectors' values into account in contrast to cosine's property of only observing the angle between two vectors ignoring their lengths. After all, two lists of NEs were created for each of the types PER, LOC, ORG and MISC, one by cosine and one by Dice similarity. Adding NE types to HeiNER makes it a valuable resource for multilingual NERC providing a fair amount of training material in various languages.

6 Acknowledgements

Thanks to Anette Frank for her suggestions and support for the thesis that is the basis of this paper.

References

Oliver Bender, Franz Josef Och, and Hermann Ney. 2003. Maximum entropy models for named entity recognition. In *Proceedings of the seventh conference on Natural language learning at HLT-NAACL 2003*, pages 148–151, Morristown, NJ, USA. Association for Computational Linguistics.

Razvan Bunescu and Marius Paşca. 2006. Using encyclopedic knowledge for named entity disambiguation. In *Proceedings of the 11th Conference of the European Chapter of the Association for Computational Linguistics (EACL-06), Trento, Italy*, pages 9–16, April.

Christian Federmann and Sabine Hunsicker. 2011. Stochastic parse tree selection for an existing rbmt system. In *Proceedings of the Sixth Workshop on Statistical Machine Translation*, pages 351–357, Edinburgh, Scotland, July. Association for Computational Linguistics.

Michael Fleischman and Eduard Hovy. 2002. Fine grained classification of named entities. In *Proceedings of the 19th international conference on Computational linguistics*, pages 1–7, Morristown, NJ, USA. Association for Computational Linguistics.

Ralph Grishman and Beth Sundheim. 1996. Message understanding conference: A brief history. In *Proceedings of the 16th International Conference on Computational Linguistics (COLING)*, pages 466–471. http://acl.ldc.upenn.edu/C/C96/C96-1079.pdf.

David Nadeau and Satoshi Sekine. 2007. A survey of named entity recognition and classification. *Linguisticae Investigationes*, 30(1):3–26, January.

Erik F. Tjong Kim Sang and Fien De Meulder. 2003. Introduction to the CoNLL-2003 Shared Task: Language-independent Named Entity Recognition. In *Proceedings of the 7th Conference on Natural language Learning at HLT-NAACL 2003*, pages 142–147, Morristown, NJ, USA.

Erik F. Tjong Kim Sang. 2002. Introduction to the CoNLL-2002 shared task: Language-independent named entity recognition. In *Proceedings of Conference on Natural Language Learning*.

G. Szarvas, R. Farkas, A. Kocsor, et al. 2006. A multilingual named entity recognition system using boosting and c4. 5 decision tree learning algorithms. *Lecture Notes in Computer Science*, 4265:267.

Wolodja Wentland, Johannes Knopp, Carina Silberer, and Matthias Hartung. 2008. Building a multilingual lexical resource for named entity disambiguation, translation and transliteration. In European Language Resources Association (ELRA), editor, *Proceedings of the Sixth International Language Resources and Evaluation (LREC'08)*, Marrakech, Morocco, may.

Author Index

Association for Computational Linguistics
209 N. Eighth Street
Stroudsburg, Pennsylvania 18360

CURRAN ASSOCIATES INC
proceedings.com